NORTHSTAR

LISTENING AND SPEAKING
Advanced

D1450178

SECOND EDITION

Sherry Preiss

Series Editors
Frances Boyd
Carol Numrich

Longman

**NorthStar: Listening and Speaking, Advanced, Second Edition
Teacher's Manual and Achievement Tests**

Pearson Education, 10 Bank Street, White Plains, NY 10606

Teacher's Manual by Sarah Lynn
Achievement Tests by Dawn Schmid

Test consultant: Tay Lesley

Development director: Penny Laporte
Project manager: Debbie Sistino
Senior development editor: Paula H. Van Ells
Vice president, director of design and production: Rhea Banker
Executive managing editor: Linda Moser
Production coordinator: Melissa Leyva
Senior production editor: Kathleen Silloway
Production editor: Jane Townsend
Director of manufacturing: Patrice Fraccio
Senior manufacturing buyer: Dave Dickey
Cover design: Rhea Banker
Text design: Quorum Creative Services
Text composition: TSI Graphics
Text font: 11/13 Sabon

ISBN 0-201-78845-4

LONGMAN ON THE **WEB**

Longman.com offers online resources for
teachers and students. Access our Companion
Websites, our online catalog, and our local
offices around the world.

Visit us at **longman.com.**

Printed in the United States of America
5 6 7 8 9 10—TCS—09 08 07 06 05

Contents

Contents

Achievement Tests

Introduction to Achievement Tests   127

Achievement Tests

UNIT **1**   T1-1

UNIT **2**   T2-1

UNIT **3**   T3-1

UNIT **4**   T4-1

UNIT **5**   T5-1

UNIT **6**   T6-1

UNIT **7**   T7-1

UNIT **8**   T8-1

UNIT **9**   T9-1

UNIT **10**   T10-1

Achievement Tests:
Test 1 Audioscript   129

Achievement Tests:
Test 1 Answer Key   139

Introduction to the *NorthStar* Series

The *NorthStar* Approach to Language Teaching   *NorthStar* is a five-level, integrated skills series for language learning. The series is divided into two strands: listening and speaking, and reading and writing. There are five books in each strand, taking students from the high beginning level of the *Introductory Student Book* to the advanced level of the *Advanced Student Book*. At each level, the two strands explore different aspects of the same contemporary themes. Each book practices language-learning skills through high-interest thematic content.

In addition to the Student Books, the *Writing Activity Book* for each level of the reading and writing strand expands and reinforces the writing process. The *Audio Program* includes, on CD or cassette, all the reading and listening segments as well as pronunciation exercises. The *Video Program* includes 3- to 5-minute segments for each unit. The segments are thematically linked to the units in the Student Books to offer additional material for listening comprehension and discussion or writing.

Integrated skills are at the heart of the **NorthStar** series. When two or more language skills are integrated, language learning is apt to be more authentic, natural, and motivating. Integrating skills offers more opportunity for recycling and reinforcing key vocabulary, grammatical structures, and ideas. As a result, students have more occasions to assimilate information and language, thereby facilitating learning.

Approach to Reading and Writing   *NorthStar* supports the approach that learning to be a good writer means learning to be a good reader and vice versa. Reading skills are taught *implicitly* throughout each unit. For example, the comprehension exercises are designed to give practice in reading skills, such as predicting, identifying main ideas and details, skimming and scanning.

Writing skills are taught *implicitly* through the readings: The readings serve as models of good writing. In the Style section, writing skills are taught *explicitly* through analysis, explanation, and guided practice.

The writing process begins at the start of each unit (often with the first Prediction exercise), continues through the unit (with dialogues, written reactions to a partner's comments, chart completion, note taking), includes the Style section (with explicit writing skills and structured practice), and culminates in the Writing Topics section, where students are asked to produce a complete piece of writing.

Reading and writing skills—including strategies for improving vocabulary, comprehension, and grammar—are cultivated in every section of every unit. In the Research Topics section, the reading and writing integration becomes most clear and relevant, as students are asked to conduct research and read texts from a variety of authentic sources and then integrate ideas from these sources into their own writing.

Approach to Listening and Speaking

NorthStar provides structured opportunities for students to practice listening to many types of discourse. Listening skills are taught *implicitly* throughout each unit. For example, the comprehension exercises are designed to give practice in such listening skills as predicting, identifying main ideas and details, and note taking.

Speaking skills are taught *implicitly* through the listenings: The listenings serve as models of functional language or conventional style. In the Style section, speaking skills are taught *explicitly* though analysis, explanation, a carefully structured pronunciation syllabus, and guided practice. The teaching of speaking begins at the start of each unit (often with the first Prediction exercise), continues through the unit (with categorizing and ranking activities, interviews, games, pronunciation practice, comparing answers and discussing differences, sharing opinions), includes the Style section (with explicit functional skills and structured practice), and culminates in the Speaking Topics section, where students use their speaking skills to create role plays, case studies, debates, radio announcements, and presentations.

Listening and speaking skills—including learning strategies for improving vocabulary, comprehension, and grammar—are cultivated in every section of every unit. In the Research Topics section, the listening and speaking integration becomes most clear and relevant as students are asked to conduct projects such as surveys or in-person and telephone interviews and then integrate ideas from these sources into their own oral presentations.

Approach to Grammar

Content drives the organization of the grammar syllabus. Accordingly, students have opportunities to encounter and work with grammar structures in authentic contexts. The purpose of the Grammar section is to enable clear and accurate discussion and writing about the unit theme.

The Grammar section of each unit is not intended to be an exhaustive treatment of a grammatical point. Rather, it is an opportunity for students to focus on a new or familiar point within the specific context of the unit. Teachers and students can use the Grammar section either as the first step in presenting a particular structure or as a review. For more detailed explanations of the grammar points, a chart of Grammar Book References is included in the Student Books. This chart cross-references the unit grammar to appropriate sections in two successful grammar series: Azar's grammar series and *Focus on Grammar*.

Grammar is taught both inductively (through discovery) and deductively (through explanation). First, students answer questions to discover the form, usage, and meaning of the grammar. Next, they read an explanation of the point, with examples in the thematic context of the unit. Finally, students practice the structures in exercises related to the content of the unit.

Approach to Vocabulary

Vocabulary practice has been increased in the Second Edition of *NorthStar.* Vocabulary is taught both *directly* and *indirectly.* Specific vocabulary exercises focus on meaning, usage, and word forms. In many of the other exercises (grammar, style, speaking and writing topics, research), the vocabulary reappears but is not the focus of the exercise.

In Section 1, Focus on the Topic, vocabulary has been chosen for its relevance in discussing the topic/theme. In other cases, the vocabulary is essential for comprehension of a listening or reading text, so the focus becomes preteaching vocabulary for comprehension. In Section 3, Focus on Vocabulary, the work takes on a different focus, as words are reviewed and studied in more depth. In this section, students are asked to go beyond the vocabulary presented in the text and explore new items. In the listening and speaking strand, a particular effort has been made to focus on idiomatic and informal expressions that are common in spoken English.

Correction in Oral Work
Students with academic and/or career goals need and want correction. You should listen to what students are saying on two levels: form and content. Use correction to help students close the gap between what they want to say and what they are able to say. Cued self-correction is preferable. Self-correction can be promoted in several ways. You will want to vary your strategies depending on the activity and time available.

- **On-the-spot correction:** As students are talking, you can use a nonverbal gesture (such as raising a finger, pulling an earlobe, writing the error on the board) to indicate that a correction is necessary.

- **Individual notes:** You may want to write down individual student's errors on a chart to have them corrected when the activity is finished. For example, in the Sample Error Chart below, general feedback is on the left-hand side. You can use symbols such as ↑ to mean "above average," → to mean "average," and ↓ to mean "below average." Specific feedback is on the right-hand side. An index card, divided into three equal parts, also works well.

Name _Maria R_	**Class** _English 101_	
General Feedback Fluency ↑ Accuracy → Pronunciation ↓	**Pronunciation/Stress** _these_ /ð/ _think_ /θ/	**Grammar/Vocabulary** _Yesterday, they say_ . . . _The students works together_ . . .
Notes _Interesting ideas about education._ _Be sure to speak loudly, too._ _Eye contact was much better._	_rural_ /r/ _official_ _product_	_They have much problems_ . . . _They needed a material subject._

- **Collective notes:** You may want to take notes that can be used later to create an error-correction exercise.

- **Tapes and transcriptions:** You may want to use tapes and transcriptions to increase students' awareness of language errors. Audiotaping student conversations and reports is especially useful in the pronunciation activities in Sections 4A and 4D, where students have an opportunity for extensive oral production. First, tape the conversation, role play, or report; then record your feedback, modeling correct pronunciation. You can also transcribe a portion for use as an error-correction activity. Use blanks or underscoring to indicate errors; then have students correct their mistakes and encourage them to appreciate how their language is improving. Occasionally, it may be interesting to have students transcribe small bits of their own language for the same purpose.

If possible, you may want to videotape an activity. Play it back and elicit oral and written comments about students' own language and their feelings about seeing themselves speaking English. Follow this with some error correction on the board.

- **Fluency line:** Students need to develop fluency. The following activity develops fluency by giving students a chance to repeat the same story, explanation, or opinion to several different people.

  Divide the class in half. Have Group B students line up, side by side, and then have Group A students line up opposite them. Each Group A student then tells the Group B student opposite him or her a story, explanation, or opinion, depending on the assignment. Time the Group A students, giving them a set amount of time to talk. The Group A students must not stop talking, and the Group B students must not interrupt, except to ask for clarification. When you signal, all Group A students must take a step to the right and repeat their comments to their next Group B partner. (The Group A student at the end of the line has to walk around to the far left to find his or her new partner.) The activity continues with you signaling each partner to change. You can speed up the process by incrementally reducing the amount of time between partners. At a designated point, the roles are reversed so that Group B students have an opportunity to talk, and Group A students have an opportunity to listen.

  The format of this activity can be modified. For example, you could have students line up in concentric circles instead of lines or have them walk freely around the room, talking with different partners.

- **Audio journal:** An audio journal is like a written journal except that students record their ideas on an audio cassette tape instead of on paper. There are a number of assignments that can lead to audio journals—for example, comments on topics discussed in class, reports on individual research, and first drafts of oral presentations. Some teachers like to have students record pronunciation exercises as a way to individualize error correction. For all these activities, it is important to specify how long the students should speak and whether they should read prepared comments or speak extemporaneously. When you receive the audio journals, you can give students feedback by recording a reply right after their comments. When replying, be sure to discuss both content and form.

A Message from the Series Editors

We think of a good textbook as a musical score or a movie script. It tells you the moves and roughly how quickly and in-what sequence to make them. But until you and your students bring it to life, a book is silent and static, a mere possibility. We hope that *NorthStar* orients, guides, and interests you as teachers.

It is our hope that the *NorthStar* series stimulates your students' thinking, which in turn stimulates their language learning, and that they will have many opportunities to reflect on the viewpoints of journalists, commentators, researchers, other students, and people in the community. Further, we hope that *NorthStar* guides them to develop their own point of view on the many and varied themes encompassed by this series.

We welcome your comments and questions. Please send them to us at the publisher:

Frances Boyd and Carol Numrich, Series Editors
NorthStar
Pearson Education
10 Bank Street
White Plains, NY 10606

Overview of the *Teacher's Manual and Achievement Tests*

The *NorthStar Teacher's Manual* includes:

- Specific suggestions for teaching each unit, including:
    - ✓ Unit-by-unit overview (scope and sequence) and summary
    - ✓ Unit-by-unit description of the Focus, Setup, and Expansion/Homework activities for each exercise
    - ✓ Suggested teaching times
    - ✓ Cross-references to the companion strand, Grammar Book References, *Writing Activity Book,* Video, and Companion Website
- The Answer Key to the Student Book
- Reproducible Achievement Tests with Answer Keys—including the test audioscript and test audio CD for the *Listening and Speaking* strand; and a test-generating CD-ROM to allow teachers to customize and adapt the 300 test items and writing tasks on the Reading and Writing Achievement Tests for the *Reading and Writing* strand
- An alphabetized-by-unit word list of the key vocabulary items practiced in each unit

COURSE PLANNER

Each unit contains approximately eight hours of classroom material, plus expansion, homework, and support material. Teachers can customize the units by assigning some exercises for homework and/or eliminating others. To help teachers customize the units for their specific teaching situation, the Unit-by-Unit Teaching Suggestions in the *Teacher's Manual* include 1, 2, or 3 stars to indicate the relative importance of each section or exercise:

✪✪✪ **Essential** sections
✪✪ **Recommended** sections
✪ **Optional** sections

To use *NorthStar* most effectively, see the teaching guide below.

CLASS TIME AVAILABLE PER UNIT	SECTIONS TO COMPLETE
8 hours or more	Essential (✪✪✪), Recommended (✪✪), Optional (✪)
6 hours	Essential (✪✪✪), Recommended (✪✪)
4 hours	Essential (✪✪✪) only

The Internet and Other Addictions

OVERVIEW

Theme:	Addictions

Listenings:	Listening One: *Interview with an Internet Addiction Counselor*
	     An interview with a psychologist
	Listening Two: *Time to Do Everything but Think*
	     An interview with a commentator

Critical Thinking Skills:	Distinguish between notions of addiction and compulsion Infer word meaning from context Recognize personal assumptions about technology Infer information not explicit in the interviews Compare and contrast differing viewpoints Support opinions with information from the interviews Hypothesize another's point of view
Listening Tasks:	Take notes on main ideas using a graphic organizer Take notes on supporting details using a graphic organizer Interpret speaker's word usage and tone Relate listenings to personal values, experiences, and opinions Identify connecting theme in two interviews Identify emphasized words in speech Locate a support group through telephone inquiries
Speaking Tasks:	Make predictions Express and defend opinions Retell a storyline from a cartoon Act out a scripted conversation Use new vocabulary in a guided conversation Use functional language to build on others' ideas Respond extemporaneously to prompts Simulate discussion sessions at a psychology conference Conduct a survey and report survey findings
Pronunciation:	Highlighting important words
Vocabulary:	Context clues Definitions Synonyms Idiomatic expressions Word forms
Grammar:	Wish statements—expressing unreality

UNIT SUMMARY

This unit deals with Internet addiction and whether it can be considered a true addiction. Listening One is an interview with a counselor who treats college students who spend endless hours with their computers. Listening Two is an interview with a writer who argues that people today are bombarded by communication and don't have time to reflect and develop their creativity.

The companion unit in *NorthStar: Reading and Writing* deals with the life story of a baseball player, Mickey Mantle, who suffered from alcoholism, a destructive addiction.

1 Focus on the Topic, PAGE 1

✪✪✪A PREDICTING

Suggested Time: 5 minutes 🕐

Focus

To get students thinking about the theme of the unit based on the title, the cartoon, and students' knowledge of addiction support groups.

Setup

Ask students to read the title and the cartoon. Have students pair up with a neighboring classmate to discuss their responses. Have pairs report back to the class.

Expansion/Homework

You may want to discuss student responses as a class.

✪✪B SHARING INFORMATION

Suggested Time: 20 minutes 🕐

Focus

To encourage free discussion of students' knowledge of and experience with addiction.

Setup

Have students form groups (with students of varying ages and backgrounds, if possible) to make a list of addictions and discuss the questions. Have the groups share their lists and any interesting insights or ideas with the class.

Expansion/Homework

You may want to discuss question 3 as a class. You could draw an octopus on the board. Point out its eight long arms and suggest how difficult it would be to get all eight arms tucked under the covers at the same time. Then have students relate that image to controlling one's multiple addictions. Discuss the questions in the book.

Link to *NorthStar: Reading and Writing*
Students using the companion text may want to discuss Mickey Mantle in response to question 2 (describing an addict).

✪✪✪ C   PREPARING TO LISTEN

BACKGROUND
Suggested Time: 15 minutes 🕐

Focus
To give students more information about the nature of addictions and the impact of Internet use on college students; to awaken interest in and aid comprehension of the listening that follows.

Setup
Have students read the text individually. Check comprehension by asking, *What is an addiction? Can support groups help compulsive Internet users? How does increasing computer use affect social behavior?* Then have students read and react to the statements individually before they form pairs to discuss their opinions. During this activity, encourage students to discuss their ideas fully, challenging any assumptions they may make about addictions and addicts.

Expansion/Homework
(1) If class time is limited, you may want to assign the reading as homework. In class, students can share their opinions. (2) You could convert this into a listening exercise by reading the text aloud as students listen. Check their comprehension with the questions listed in Setup. (3) This reading can be used as an information gap activity. Photocopy the text and then cut out the paragraphs. Pair stronger and weaker students. Give each student a different paragraph to read and have them take notes. With only notes in hand, have students explain their paragraphs to their partners. To check comprehension, have students respond to the questions listed in Setup. (4) To add challenge to the discussion, insist that the students come to a consensus on statements 3, 4, and 5 on page 3. (5) Encourage your students to follow this topic in the news or online. Have them bring to class any articles they find that mention addiction.

VOCABULARY FOR COMPREHENSION
Suggested Time: 15 minutes 🕐

Focus
To acquaint students with vocabulary that is often used when discussing addictions and the Internet; to aid comprehension of the listening.

Setup

Review the pronunciation of the words or expressions before students complete the exercise independently. Go over the answers as a class, with students reading them aloud so you can correct pronunciation.

Expansion/Homework

(1) If class time is limited, you may want to assign the exercise as homework and use class time to check answers and correct pronunciation. (2) To help students memorize vocabulary, have them work in pairs to quiz each other on the definitions. One can play the teacher; the other can play the student. Then have them switch roles.

2 Focus On Listening, PAGE 4

✪✪✪ A | **LISTENING ONE:** *Interview with an Internet Addiction Counselor*

Suggested Time: 10 minutes ⏱

Focus

To help students predict the contents of the interview; to present an interview with a psychologist about the symptoms of an increasing phenomenon: Internet addiction.

Setup

Have students listen to the beginning of the interview and then write three questions they expect the interviewer to ask. Invite students to share their questions as you write them on the board. Encourage them to use the vocabulary introduced in the previous section by writing the list of words on the board.

Expansion/Homework

If some of the students' questions remain unanswered after the interview, ask them to imagine how Dr. Jonathan Kandell might respond.

✪✪✪ LISTENING FOR MAIN IDEAS

Suggested Time: 20 minutes ⏱

Focus

To help students listen for the main ideas in an extended interview.

Setup

Have students read the prompts before listening. Play the interview only once. Have students take notes as they listen. Then in pairs, have students compare their notes about the main ideas.

Expansion/Homework

You may want students to wait to compare their notes about the main ideas until after they have finished the Listening for Details activity. Students might allocate different information as *main* or *detailed*. If all the information is written first, it is easier to sift through it and identify main concepts and then details.

✪✪✪ LISTENING FOR DETAILS
Suggested Time: 20 minutes ⏱

Focus
To get students to listen again, this time for specific pieces of information.

Setup
First have students write the details they remember. Play the interview again. Have students compare their notes with a classmate. If disagreements arise, replay the interview rather than give the answer. In some cases, students may even want to listen a third time.

Expansion/Homework
You could have students use their notes to write a summary of the interview.

Link to *NorthStar: Reading and Writing*
Ask your students using the companion text to read their notes about the symptoms and warning signs of addiction and think about what happened to Mickey Mantle's social skills as he became addicted to alcohol.

✪✪ REACTING TO THE LISTENING
Suggested Time: 25 minutes ⏱

Focus
To encourage students to interpret tone of voice and word choice to determine a speaker's attitude; to promote critical discussion of and reflection on the interview; to encourage students to think of and consider several possibilities in their responses.

Setup
For Exercise 1, have the students read the questions before listening to each excerpt. Allow them a few minutes to think about their responses before discussing them with a partner. If there is disagreement, welcome it. Encourage students to support their points of view with details from the listening. To enrich this discussion, try to pair students from different cultural backgrounds and varying ages. For Exercise 2, lead the class discussion.

Expansion/Homework
(1) To teach students to infer meaning and look for a range of answers, you may want to do the first excerpt as a class before playing the others. Encourage a range of responses by writing all students' ideas on the board. Emphasize that it is possible for students to have varying opinions as long as their reasoning is sound. (2) You could expand question 2 by asking students to role play an interview between an addiction counselor and a client with a possible Internet addiction. Ask students, *What kinds of questions would the counselor ask to identify whether this person is addicted? How would an addict (versus a heavy user) respond?* After students have brainstormed questions and responses, have them do the role play in pairs.

✪✪✪ B **LISTENING TWO:** *Time to Do Everything but Think*

Suggested Time: 25 minutes 🕐

Focus

To listen to an interview that explores the broader impact Internet use and electronic communications have on one's mind.

Setup

Have students read the prompts before listening. Play the interview as many times as necessary for students to take notes. Have students of varying levels work together in pairs to compare their notes. For Exercise 2, have students read and react to the statements independently before they form small groups to discuss their answers. Encourage students to support their points of view with details from the interview.

✪✪✪ C **LINKING LISTENINGS ONE AND TWO**

Suggested Time: 25 minutes 🕐

Focus

To get students to remember and synthesize information; to reflect on opinions presented in the two interviews.

Setup

Have students complete the chart independently and then form small groups (with students from different language backgrounds, if possible) to discuss their opinions. Encourage students to support their opinions with information from the interviews. In the same groups, have students read the cartoon and respond to the questions in Exercise 2.

Expansion/Homework

To promote active use of new words, you may want to list the vocabulary from Section 1C (Vocabulary for Comprehension) on the board. If students are using the companion text, *NorthStar: Reading and Writing*, you may also want to include vocabulary from that unit's Section 1C on the board. Or you could create a list integrating the vocabulary from the Listening/Speaking and the Reading/Writing strands. See the Word List for each unit at the end of the Teacher's Manual and on the Companion Website at **http://www.longman.com/northstar**.

Link to *NorthStar: Reading and Writing*

For Exercise 1, question 1, ask students, *How does the example of Mickey Mantle's alcoholism compare in severity to the damage caused by Internet addiction?*

3 Focus on Vocabulary, PAGE 10

✪ EXERCISE 1
Suggested Time: 15 minutes ⏲

Focus
To reinforce unit vocabulary; to expand students' vocabulary by deriving variations in word forms.

Setup
Have students of similar fluency levels work in small groups to complete the exercise. Encourage them to consult each other and their dictionaries before consulting you. Remind students that there may be multiple answers for some word forms, but that the class is seeking the most commonly used forms. Check the answers as a class, reviewing the pronunciation of the words.

Expansion/Homework
If class time is limited, you may want to assign this section as homework and use class time to check answers and work on pronunciation.

✪ EXERCISE 2
Suggested Time: 15 minutes ⏲

Focus
To apply vocabulary in this unit to a new context: a conversation among women addicted to shopping.

Setup
Divide the class into groups of three. Ask students to read the whole conversation before filling in the blanks. Encourage students to role play the conversation with drama and enthusiasm. If students are involved in their dramatizations, have volunteer groups perform them for the class.

Expansion/Homework
You could ask students to create a similar conversation among Internet or gambling addicts. They can perform their dialogues for the class.

✪ EXERCISE 3
Suggested Time: 15 minutes ⏲

Focus
To apply vocabulary in this unit to a new context: a paragraph about an addict.

Setup
This exercise may be assigned for homework and then presented to small groups in class. Some students may prefer to submit the paragraph directly to you.

Link to *NorthStar: Reading and Writing*
Students using the companion text may want to describe Mickey Mantle in this writing assignment.

✪ EXERCISE 4
Suggested Time: 20 minutes 🕐

Focus

To give more practice defining and using the vocabulary in this unit.

Setup

As a class, practice pronouncing the underlined words and expressions. Students can do this exercise for homework and then compare their answers with a partner in class.

Expansion/Homework

To help students memorize vocabulary, have them work in pairs to quiz each other on the definitions. One is the teacher. The other is the student. Then they switch roles.

✪ EXERCISE 5
Suggested Time: 15 minutes 🕐

Focus

To give structured practice applying the vocabulary from this unit in a guided conversation.

Setup

Give students a few minutes of preparation time to take notes before they divide into pairs to ask and answer the questions using the key words listed. To take advantage of the conversational tone of this exercise, remind students to make lots of eye contact with each other.

Expansion/Homework

After the in-class activity, students could write their responses in paragraphs or compose final spoken responses to you in their audio journals.

 For extra vocabulary practice, have students work on the self-grading vocabulary activities for the unit on the NorthStar Companion Website at **http://www.longman.com/northstar**.

4 Focus on Speaking, PAGE 14

✪✪A PRONUNCIATION: Highlighting Important Words
Suggested Time: 20 minutes 🕐

Focus

To practice shifting pitch and vowel stress in order to add emphasis to certain words.

Setup

Read the introductory passage aloud or have students read silently. Instead of playing the audio, you may want to demonstrate the examples yourself. For Exercise 1, have the class listen to the sentences and then circle the words that are stressed. Have students pair up (with students from different language backgrounds, if possible) to practice pronouncing the sentences. With the same partner, have students read the dialogue in Exercise 2 and highlight the stressed words. Then have them practice the dialogue with their partners.

Expansion/Homework

Have the pairs of students present their dialogues to the class. Encourage students to exaggerate the variation in pitch and vowel stress.

✪✪ B GRAMMAR: Wish Statements—Expressing Unreality

Suggested Time: 25 minutes 🕐

Focus

To practice using wish statements and express unreality when talking about addictions.

Setup

Have students work in pairs (with students from different language backgrounds, if possible) to examine the dialogues and answer the questions that follow. Ask students to read the grammar explanations silently. Respond to any questions and point out how *wish* and *would* are both stressed in short-answer responses. Model Exercise 2 so that students understand that Student A has the correct information and that Student B must cover the information and only listen to the prompt. When the pairs finish the first part, have them switch roles.

Expansion/Homework

(1) The first part of this section works well for homework. You can answer questions in class before students pair up for Exercise 2. (2) For further practice, offer exercises from *Focus on Grammar, Advanced* and from Azar's *Understanding and Using English Grammar.* See the Grammar Book References on page 247 of the Student Book.

✪✪✪ C STYLE: Expressions for Building on Others' Ideas

Suggested Time: 25 minutes 🕐

Focus

To guide students in ways to build on one another's ideas; to model collaborative conversations.

Setup

Ask students to read the list of expressions. Pair stronger and weaker students to practice using the expressions. Remind students that this is an exercise in collaboration and that they should agree no matter what their personal opinions are.

 For extra listening practice, have students use the NorthStar Companion Video.

✪✪✪ D SPEAKING TOPIC

Focus

To integrate the concepts, vocabulary, pronunciation skills (highlighting important words), grammar (wish statements), and style focus (building on another's ideas) of the unit in a simulation.

Setup

Divide the class into three groups and decide which session each group will role play. Have each group assign a note taker and a group leader to facilitate the discussion. Give a time limit of 15 minutes for the discussions. Then have each group report the main points of their session to the class.

Expansion/Homework

(1) As students speak, circulate around the room listening. Note pronunciation and usage errors. At the end of the activity, present your notes—either for the class or for each individual student—and have students correct the errors. Help students work on pronunciation. (2) Each group could do a short five-minute demonstration of its discussion. The rest of the class can watch and note all the expressions for building on others' ideas they heard during the session. You can also note errors and do a short error-correction review before the next group begins.

✪ E RESEARCH TOPICS

Focus

To raise students' consciousness about diagnosis and support services for addicts; to practice survey and reporting skills by conducting a survey on an addiction.

Setup

Have students work individually or in pairs to find an Internet-addiction support group. Have them report and reflect on their findings. For the survey activity, have students form pairs of their own choosing to adapt the survey and conduct interviews. Students can summarize their findings and present them to the class.

Expansion/Homework

(**1**) If you live in an English-speaking environment, you might want to invite a representative of any addict support group to speak to the class about its mission and method. Each student can write at least one question to pose to the guest. You may want to review their questions as a class to eliminate redundancy. (**2**) For further reading on this topic, the following texts are recommended: *Caught in the Net: How to Recognize the Signs of Internet Addiction—And a Winning Strategy for Success,* by Kimberly Young; *Life on the Screen*, by Sherry Turkle; and *Virtual Addiction: Help for Netheads, Cyberfreaks, and Those Who Love Them,* by David N. Greenfield, Ph.D.

Link to *NorthStar: Reading and Writing*

If time allows, you could do a writing topic from Section 4C (at home) and a speaking topic (in class). You will probably want to choose the research topic that fits your students and the classroom environment best. When students speak, remind them to use examples and vocabulary from the Reading/Writing unit on addictions.

UNIT 2

Celebration, Florida: Disney's Utopia

OVERVIEW	
Theme:	Utopian Movements
Listenings:	Listening One: *The Celebration Experiment* 　　An interview with a scholar of American Studies Listening Two: *Living in Celebration* 　　An interview with a resident journalist
Critical Thinking Skills:	Recognize personal assumptions about community Classify information Infer word meaning from context Infer meaning not explicit in the text Hypothesize scenarios Compare and contrast viewpoints Make judgments Analyze relationships between ideas
Listening Tasks:	Identify main ideas Listen for details Interpret speaker's attitude and tone of voice Relate listening to personal values Take notes on supporting details using a graphic organizer Synthesize information from two interviews Identify words spoken with reduced pronunciation View and critique a movie
Speaking Tasks:	Make predictions Summarize ideas Express conjecture with appropriate words and phrases Role play a conversation using new vocabulary Voice opinions using opening words and phrases Practice the role of a discussion leader Simulate a town meeting Present a two-minute movie review Conduct an interview and report results
Pronunciation:	Reduction of *as*, *has*, and *is*
Vocabulary:	Context clues Synonyms and definitions Analogies
Grammar:	Noun clauses after verbs or expressions of urgency

UNIT SUMMARY

This unit introduces Celebration, USA, an ideal community designed by Disney. In two interviews, students learn from former residents about the quality of life in Celebration and how the ideals of community life did not match its realities. The first interview is with Professor Andrew Ross, who, after living in Celebration for one year, wrote a book about his experience. The second interview is with *New York Times* journalist Douglas Frantz and his wife, Catherine Collins, who lived with their children in Celebration for two years.

The companion unit in *NorthStar: Reading and Writing* explores the history of American utopian movements and presents a critique of the life of the working poor in contemporary U.S. society.

1 Focus on the Topic, PAGE 23

✪✪✪A PREDICTING

Suggested Time: 5 minutes 🕐

Focus
To get students thinking about the appeal of a contemporary utopian community; to predict the content of the unit based on the title and the photograph.

Setup
Ask students to read the title and paragraph and look at the photographs. Have students pair up with a neighboring classmate to discuss their predictions. Have pairs report back to the class.

Expansion/Homework
You may want to do this section as a class by eliciting responses and writing them on the board. Students may enjoy returning to their predictions after they learn more about Celebration.

✪✪B SHARING INFORMATION

Suggested Time: 20 minutes 🕐

Focus
To get students to identify the features they seek in a community; to encourage free discussion of the attributes of various communities.

Setup
Ask students to read the directions and items in the list. Clarify new vocabulary. Have students work individually to identify what they value most. Then have students share their answers with a partner (someone from a different language background, if possible).

Expansion/Homework

(1) For a follow-up activity and brief discussion, ask, *Did you and your partner choose the same features? If you had to agree with your partner on five feature for an ideal living community, which five would you choose?* (2) Students could compare their actual communities to their ideal communites. Ask, *Which of these features does your community have?*

✪✪✪ C PREPARING TO LISTEN

BACKGROUND
Suggested Time: 15 minutes ⏲

Focus
To set the historical context of utopian movements in the United States; to awaken interest in and aid student comprehension of the listening that follows.

Setup
Have students read the timeline with a partner. Clarify new vocabulary. Model this classification exercise. Give a brief summary of one of the utopian movements and then identify its central themes. You may need to clarify the concept of *community*, which in this context means *connection to others*. Have students work with their partners to summarize the remaining movements and identify their central themes.

Expansion/Homework
(1) If class time is limited, you may want to assign the reading as homework. In class, students can work in pairs to classify the utopian movements. (2) This reading can be easily converted into a jigsaw: Photocopy the text and then cut out the paragraphs. Pair stronger and weaker students together. Give each student a different paragraph to read and take notes on. With only notes in hand, have students explain their paragraphs to their partners. (3) Encourage your students to follow this topic in the news or online. Have them bring to class any articles that mention Celebration, Florida, or other "ideal" communities.

VOCABULARY FOR COMPREHENSION
Suggested Time: 15 minutes ⏲

Focus
To acquaint students with vocabulary used when discussing communities; to aid comprehension of the listening.

Setup
Have students individually read the fictional Web page. Review the pronunciation of the italicized words embedded in the text. Ask students to work with a partner to match the words with their related expressions. Go over the answers as a class, with students reading them aloud so you can correct pronunciation.

Expansion/Homework

(1) If class time is limited, you may want to assign the exercise as homework and use class time to check answers and correct pronunciation. (2) To help students memorize vocabulary, have them work in pairs to quiz each other on the definitions. One can play the teacher; the other can play the student. Then have them switch roles.

2 Focus on Listening, PAGE 28

✪✪✪ A | LISTENING ONE: *The Celebration Experiment*

Suggested Time: 10 minutes ⏱

Focus

To help students predict the contents of the interview; to present an interview about the quality of life in a designed urban community.

Setup

Have students read the introductory paragraph and directions. Pair students of varying ages and backgrounds to make their predictions. Encourage them to use the vocabulary introduced in the previous section by writing the list of words on the board. Have students listen to the excerpt and then check their predictions.

Expansion/Homework

You may want the whole class to make predictions, while you write the students' ideas on the board. After listening, students can check the board to see how accurate their predictions were.

✪✪✪ **LISTENING FOR MAIN IDEAS**

Suggested Time: 20 minutes ⏱

Focus

To help students listen for the main ideas in an extended interview.

Setup

Have students read the statements before listening. Play the interview only once. Have students complete the exercise. Review students' answers as a class. If there is disagreement, have students listen to the interview again.

Expansion/Homework

To add challenge, convert this into a note-taking activity. After students read the statements, have them close their books and take notes on a divided page: Main Ideas/Details. Then students can open their books and use their notes to complete the exercise.

✪✪✪ LISTENING FOR DETAILS
Suggested Time: 20 minutes 🕐

Focus
To get students to listen again, this time for specific pieces of information.

Setup
Play the interview again. Then have students complete the exercise individually. Pair neighboring classmates to compare answers. If disagreements arise, replay the interview rather than give the answer. In some cases, students may even want to listen a third time.

Expansion/Homework
Convert this into a listening/speaking exercise. Read the true/false statements orally. Have the class discuss whether they are true or false. If students are unable to decide, replay the interview rather than give the answer.

✪✪ REACTING TO THE LISTENING
Suggested Time: 25 minutes 🕐

Focus
To encourage students to interpret tone of voice and word choice to determine a speaker's attitude; to promote critical discussion of and reflection on the interview.

Setup
For Exercise 1, have the students read the questions before listening to each excerpt. As they listen, have them write notes and key words. Allow them a few minutes to think about their responses before discussing them with a partner. Encourage students to support their points of view with details from the listening. To enrich this discussion, pair students from different language backgrounds, if possible. For Exercise 2, have students independently complete their responses and then discuss their ideas with a partner (someone from a different language background, if possible).

Expansion/Homework
(1) To teach students to infer meaning, you may want to do one excerpt as a class before playing the others. Encourage a range of responses by writing all students' ideas on the board. (2) Before students speak in pairs, you could go over the intonation of the sentence starters using stress to highlight important words, just as students learned in Unit 1.

✪✪✪ B   LISTENING TWO: *Living in Celebration*
Suggested Time 25 minutes 🕐

Focus
To present an interview that deepens students' understanding of life in the designed community, Celebration.

Setup

Have students read the introductory paragraph and the chart before listening. Play the interview as many times as necessary for students to complete the chart. Have students of varying levels work together in pairs to compare their notes.

Expansion/Homework

Have students draw a map of Celebration. Let them listen to the interviews again or read the transcript to find the helpful details that will enhance their schematic map making.

✪✪✪ C ████ **LINKING LISTENINGS ONE AND TWO** ████

Suggested Time: 25 minutes 🕐

Focus

To get students to remember and synthesize information; to reflect on opinions presented in the two interviews.

Setup

Have students form small groups (with students of varying ages and backgrounds, if possible) to discuss the first question. Have students complete the chart independently and then return to their small groups to discuss their opinions. Encourage students to share their reasons with one another.

Expansion/Homework

To promote active use of new words during this activity, you may want to list the vocabulary from Section 1C (Vocabulary for Comprehension) on the board. Or you could create a list integrating the vocabulary from the Listening/Speaking and Reading/Writing strands. See the Word List for each unit at the end of the Teacher's Manual and on the Companion Website at **http://www.longman.com/northstar**.

Links to *NorthStar: Reading and Writing*

(1) Ask students, *Which of the features on the chart do you think appealed to members of Brook Farm?* (2) Ask students, *Do you think Celebration addresses any of the issues Barbara Ehrenreich raises in her book* Nickel and Dimed? *Do the features on the chart help solve the problems of the working poor? If so, how? If not, why?*

3 Focus on Vocabulary, PAGE 34

✪ **EXERCISE 1**

Suggested Time: 30 minutes 🕐

Focus

To introduce students to the concept of analogies; to reinforce unit vocabulary.

Setup

Have students read the introductory explanation. Present more examples of simple analogies (foot : leg :: hand : arm; city : urban :: country : rural) so students understand how they work. Pair students up to read and complete the analogies and then to write their rationales. Review students' work as a class.

Expansion/Homework

(1) You may want students to first complete Exercise 2, which reviews the definitions of much of this vocabulary, before they work on these analogies. (2) Give students related vocabulary to create analogies of their own.

✪ EXERCISE 2

Suggested Time: 15 minutes

Focus

To review the definitions of unit vocabulary.

Setup

Ask students to work individually to match the vocabulary. Check the answers as a class, reviewing the pronunciation of the words.

Expansion/Homework

(1) If class time is limited, you may want to assign this exercise as homework and use class time to check answers and work on pronunciation. (2) To help students memorize this vocabulary, have them work in pairs to quiz each other on the definitions. One can play the teacher; the other can play the student. Then have them switch roles.

✪ EXERCISE 3

Suggested Time: 15 minutes

Focus

To use vocabulary learned in this unit in a guided conversation.

Setup

Divide the class into pairs and assign each student a letter role (A or B). Have the B students turn to page 36 to read the list of vocabulary. Have the A students read the prompts in this exercise. If Student B is unable to identify a synonym, Student A can give a clue by saying the italicized words. If Student B still cannot identify a synonym, Student A can give the phrase. Student B will still need to use the phrase in an appropriate response to Students A's prompt.

Expansion/Homework

For homework, students could write out their responses to each statement or compose final responses in their audio journals.

 For extra vocabulary practice, have students work on the self-grading vocabulary activities for the unit on the NorthStar Companion Website at **http://www.longman.com/northstar**.

❹ Focus on Speaking, PAGE 38

✪✪A PRONUNCIATION: Reduction of *as, has,* and *is*

Suggested Time: 20 minutes 🕐

Focus
To practice listening for and pronouncing the reduced function words *as, has, is* and the *–es* plural.

Setup
Read the introductory passage aloud or have students read silently. Instead of playing the audio, you may want to demonstrate the examples yourself. For Exercise 1, have the class listen to the sentences and then write the words. Have students work in pairs (with students from different language backgrounds, if possible) to practice pronouncing these sentences. With the same partner, have students match the sentences in Exercise 2 and then practice reading them with their partners. They may need to refer to the timeline in Section 1C to complete this exercise.

Expansion/Homework
To emphasize that both types of pronunciation are correct, have students read each sentence twice, once with regular stress and once with reduced stress on the function words.

✪✪B GRAMMAR: Noun Clauses after Verbs or Expressions of Urgency

Suggested Time: 25 minutes 🕐

Focus
To have students practice noun-clause usage after verbs of urgency as they discuss Disney's town, Celebration.

Setup
Have students work in pairs (with students from different language backgrounds, if possible) to examine the sentences and answer the questions that follow. Ask students to read the grammar explanations silently. Respond to any questions before pairing up students to do Exercise 2. Model the first exchange with a volunteer student. When students finish the first part, have them switch roles.

Expansion/Homework
For further practice, offer exercises from *Focus on Grammar, Advanced* and from Azar's *Understanding and Using English Grammar.* See the Grammar Book References on page 247 of the Student Book.

Link to *NorthStar: Reading and Writing*
Have students write statements about Brook farm using the verbs and expression of urgency: *recommend, propose, demand, it was preferable, it was essential,* and *it was important.*

✪✪✪ C **STYLE: Discussing Opinions**

Suggested Time: 25 minutes 🕐

Focus

To get students to practice various phrases when asking for and expressing an opinion.

Setup

Ask students to read the information and the list of expressions, or present this information on the board. Divide the class into small groups of students of similar fluency to practice applying the expressions while discussing controversial issues. You may want to write the expressions on the board so that students don't refer to their books. Encourage them to dramatize their exchanges, using gestures and eye contact. Circulate among the pairs, listening and correcting.

Expansion/Homework

If possible, have students record these exchanges and then replay them to hear their own performances. They can listen for pronunciation and usage errors, which they may then correct.

 For extra listening practice, have students use the NorthStar Companion Video.

✪✪✪ D **SPEAKING TOPIC**

Focus

To integrate the concepts, vocabulary, pronunciation skills (reduction of *as*, *has*, and *is*), grammar (noun clauses after verbs of urgency), and style focus (discussing opinions) of the unit in a simulation of a town meeting.

Setup

Divide the class into two groups. Review the agenda with the class. Give each group ten minutes to develop arguments and designate roles. Work individually with the moderator to review the role and phrases the students may need (welcoming people to the meeting, eliciting comments and questions, encouraging negotiation, and closing the meeting). On the board, write the phrases for discussing opinions from Section 4C to encourage students to use these expressions in their role play.

Expansion/Homework

(1) As students speak, note pronunciation and usage errors. At the end of the simulation, present your notes—either for the class or for each individual student—and have students correct the errors. Help students work on pronunciation. (2) As you review the agenda, you could also solicit any other issues mentioned in the interviews that residents or the administration may want to discuss, such as privacy or lack thereof, the presence of journalists, or the cost of housing.

⊕E RESEARCH TOPICS

Focus

To view a movie that deals with living in ideal communities and to summarize the movie in a two-minute review; to explore how people experience their communities by interviewing a local resident and summarizing the findings.

Setup

Students can do these projects independently or in pairs of their own choosing. If possible, show the movie in class. Students can then compose a review of it to present in the following class. For the interviews, you may want to suggest community centers, such as a senior citizen center, a youth center, or a social club, where students might find people with the time, interest, and knowledge to discuss their communities. Students can summarize their interviews and present them to the class.

Expansion/Homework

(1) If you live in an English-speaking environment, you might want to invite a resident of the school neighborhood to speak to the class about neighborhood issues and concerns. Each student can write at least one question to pose to the guest. Before the interview, you may want to review their questions as a class to eliminate redundancy. (2) For further reading on this topic, the following texts are recommended: *Celebration, U.S.A.: Living in Disney's Brave New Town*, by Douglas Frantz and Catherine Collins; *The Celebration Chronicles: Life, Liberty, and the Pursuit of Property Value in Disney's New Town*, by Andrew Ross; and *Utopia*, by Thomas More.

Link to *NorthStar: Reading and Writing*

If time allows, you could assign a writing topic from Section 4C (at home) and a speaking topic (in class). You will probably want to choose the research topic that fits your students and the environment best. When students speak, remind them to use examples and vocabulary from the Reading/Writing unit on utopian communities.

UNIT **3**

The Bold and the Bashful

OVERVIEW	
Theme:	Personality
Listenings:	Listening One: *Americans Are Getting Shyer* 　　An interview with a professor of psychology Listening Two: *The Pollyanna Syndrome* 　　A commentary
Critical Thinking Skills:	Measure and compare personality traits Rank shyness factors Infer word meaning from context Analyze word usage Re-evaluate assumptions in light of new information Critique an argument Hypothesize another's point of view Interpret song lyrics
Listening Tasks:	Take notes on main ideas Listen for details Interpret speaker's attitude and emotions Relate listenings to personal experiences and values Identify thought groups in speech Compare and contrast intonation patterns Take dictation
Speaking Tasks:	Make predictions Express and defend opinions Construct and perform a dialogue Respond extemporaneously to prompts using new 　　vocabulary Describe one's personality using new vocabulary Practice using words and phrases to express uncertainty, 　　to break the ice, and to maintain a conversation Role play small-talk conversations Role play interviews Present research on phobias
Pronunciation:	Grouping words together
Vocabulary:	Context clues Word definitions Synonyms Idiomatic expressions Vocabulary classification
Grammar:	Adjective clauses—identifying and nonidentifying

UNIT SUMMARY

This unit deals with a cross-cultural view of shyness and other personality traits. Listening One is a surprising and funny interview with a professor of psychology who discusses the nature of shyness and the ways in which it can impede a person's happiness and success. Listening Two is an ironic commentary on the Pollyanna syndrome, a state of exaggerated optimism.

The companion unit in *NorthStar: Reading and Writing* deals with the impact of optimism and self-confidence on the pursuit of success.

1 Focus on the Topic, PAGE 47

A PREDICTING

Suggested Time: 5 minutes

Focus
To predict the content of the unit based on the title, the drawing, and students' personal experiences.

Setup
Ask students to read the title, look at the drawing, and discuss the questions with a neighboring classmate.

Expansion/Homework
In this cartoon, the shy person is standing in the background, feeling too timid to join the conversation at the picnic. You may want to ask students, *What are other ways a shy person may express his or her discomfort in a social situation? Are men apt to be shyer than women, or vice versa?*

B SHARING INFORMATION

Suggested Time: 25 minutes

Focus
To develop students' awareness of their own personality traits.

Setup
Have students take the quiz individually; then share their scores and discuss the questions in Exercise 2 in small groups.

Expansion/Homework
(1) To explore how students feel when speaking English, ask them to take the quiz twice: the first time thinking only about their native-language context, and the second time thinking only about an English-speaking context. Have them identify differences between the scores and discuss with the class any reaction they may have. (2) You may want to have students evaluate the quiz, thinking critically about its validity for them personally and across cultures.

✪✪✪ C   PREPARING TO LISTEN

BACKGROUND
Suggested Time: 15 minutes ⏱

Focus
To develop students' awareness of the number of people who experience shyness; to raise students' consciousness of the dynamic that cross-cultural communication plays in the perception and expression of shyness; to get students to consider possible factors that contribute to shyness; to awaken interest in and aid comprehension of the listening that follows.

Setup
For Exercise 1, have students with different personalities form pairs to predict the results of the survey, compare their answers to those on page 48, and discuss the questions in Exercise 2. For Exercise 3, have students work with their same partners to rate the influence of each factor. During this activity, encourage students to discuss their ideas fully, challenging any assumptions they may make about shyness or shy people. Lead a follow-up discussion. Ask, *Which factors are very important in causing shyness? Why? Which factors are not very important? Why not?*

Expansion/Homework
(1) Before the discussion, you could have the class brainstorm phrases learned in Units 1 and 2 for building on others' ideas and expressing opinions. Write the phrases on the board for students' reference during this short discussion. (2) To add challenge, insist that students come to a consensus in their rating of the top three very important factors.

VOCABULARY FOR COMPREHENSION
Suggested Time: 20 minutes ⏱

Focus
To acquaint students with vocabulary that is often used when discussing shyness and personality traits; to aid comprehension of the listening that follows.

Setup
Ask students to work individually to complete Exercises 1 and 2. After students compare answers with a partner, go over the answers as a class, with students reading them aloud so you can correct pronunciation.

Expansion/Homework
(1) You may want to assign this section as homework and use class time to check answers and work on pronunciation. (2) To help students memorize vocabulary, have them work in pairs to quiz each other on the definitions. One can act as the teacher; the other can play the student. Then have them switch roles.

2 Focus on Listening, PAGE 52

✪✪✪ A ▐ LISTENING ONE: *Americans Are Getting Shyer*
Suggested time: 10 minutes ⏱

Focus
To get students to consider the immense impact extreme shyness can have on a person's life; to help students predict the content of the interview.

Setup
Have students work with a partner to predict some problems shy people may experience. Have students listen to the excerpt and compare that list with their own. Ask students to share any reactions with the class.

Expansion/Homework
As a class, you may want to elicit ideas and write them on the board for students' reference after they listen to the excerpt.

✪✪✪ LISTENING FOR MAIN IDEAS
Suggested Time: 15 minutes ⏱

Focus
To help students listen for the main ideas in an extended interview.

Setup
Have students read the prompts before listening to Parts One and Two. Play the interview as students write their notes. Then have students compare their notes with a neighboring classmate. You may also want to review the notes as a class.

Expansion/Homework
Before you begin the listening, you may want to discuss the distinction between *cultural* and *social* factors. Cultural factors focus on the *values* of a society; social factors focus on the *social communication* and the *structure* of social units in a society.

✪✪✪ LISTENING FOR DETAILS
Suggested Time: 20 minutes ⏱

Focus
To get students to listen carefully again, this time for specific pieces of information.

Setup
First have students read the questions, supplying answers they already know. Play the interview again, letting students compare answers after each part. If disagreements arise, replay the segment rather than give the answer.

Expansion/Homework
You could have pairs of students quiz each other by reading the questions aloud. Student A can read the questions in Part One to Student B. In Part Two, have

them switch roles. To aid in their exchanges, you may want to write phrases for expressing uncertainty on the board (*I guess . . . /Perhaps . . . /I suppose . . .*).

✪✪✪ REACTING TO THE LISTENING
Suggested Time: 25 minutes 🕐

Focus
To encourage students to interpret tone of voice and word choice to determine a speaker's attitude; to promote critical discussion of and reflection on the interview.

Setup
Have the students read the questions before they listen to the excerpts. Because these passages are especially challenging, you may want to play each excerpt twice. After pairs share their ideas, analyze the excerpt as a class. For Exercise 2, allow students a few minutes to think about their responses before discussing them with small groups. If there is disagreement, welcome it. Encourage students to support their points of view with details from the listening. To enrich the discussion, try to group students of different backgrounds and varying ages. Have the group report especially interesting or insightful ideas they may have discussed to the class.

Expansion/Homework
You may want students to change partners after each excerpt.

✪✪✪ B | LISTENING TWO: *The Pollyanna Syndrome*
Suggested Time: 25 minutes 🕐

Focus
To learn about the trait of optimism; to learn idioms used to describe positive attitudes; to practice listening to an ironic and sophisticated piece of commentary.

Setup
Have students work in pairs (with students from different language backgrounds, if possible) to discuss the introductory questions. Have students read the options in Exercise 1 before playing the commentary. Have students compare their answers with a neighboring classmate before going on to Exercise 2. Read the expressions aloud in Exercise 2. Have students form pairs of their own choosing, and have them use the idioms listed to discuss times in their lives when they had to find the positive in a negative situation.

Expansion/Homework
(1) To introduce the topic, you may want to discuss the first question as a class. Make sure students understand the concept of "making lemonade out of lemons" by describing a few bad situations (crazy traffic on the way to work; no table available at your favorite restaurant; missing the bus to class) in which they try to find the positive. (2) After listening to the passages, ask students, *What is Julie*

Danis's resolution? Why does she plan to suck on some lemons? (3) This listening is quite challenging. As a final wrap up, you may want students to listen to the commentary as they read along. Stop the audio frequently to allow students to ask questions. Get students to focus on irony and tone as a key to comprehension.

Link to *NorthStar: Reading and Writing*
Students using the companion text can discuss the ways in which the main character in Reading One, "Gotta Dance," was optimistic.

✪✪✪ C   LINKING LISTENINGS ONE AND TWO

Suggested Time: 30 minutes 🕮

Focus
To get students to discuss freely their experiences with shyness, phobias, and optimism; to apply the language and ideas of this unit to two new contexts: a dialogue between a pessimist and an optimist, and a cartoon about low self-esteem.

Setup
For Exercise 1, have students of varying ages and experiences share their experiences in small groups. For Exercise 2, have students form pairs of their own choosing to perform a role play. Encourage use of eye contact and gestures to enliven the role play.

Expansion/Homework
(1) Before beginning this section, you may want to have students restate each listening in pairs, small groups, or as a class, to help strengthen their overall grasp of the material. (2) To promote active use of new words during the role play, you may want to list the vocabulary from Section 1C (Vocabulary for Comprehension) on the board. If students are using the companion text, *NorthStar: Reading and Writing*, you may also want to include vocabulary from that unit's Section 1C on the board. Or you could create a list integrating the vocabulary from the Listening/Speaking and Reading/Writing strands. See the Word List for each unit at the end of the Teacher's Manual and on the Companion Website at **http://www.longman.com/northstar**. (3) Listen as students improvise their conversations for Exercise 2 and note any errors on a divided page: Usage/Pronunciation. Have them correct the usage errors and practice correct pronunciation. Circulate around the room, answering students' questions. As a class, you can review the pronunciation of some of the most frequent errors.

Link to *NorthStar: Reading and Writing*
Ask students using the companion text, *What advice do you think Dennis O'Grady would give to the man in the cartoon in Exercise 3?*

❸ Focus on Vocabulary, PAGE 58

✪ EXERCISE 1
Suggested Time: 20 minutes 🕐

Focus

To give more practice with the idiomatic vocabulary in this unit; to apply the vocabulary to a related theme mentioned by Philip Zimbardo in Listening One—birth order theory.

Setup

As a class, practice pronouncing the words. Then have students work with a partner (someone from a different language background, if possible) to complete the exercise. Encourage them to consult each other and their dictionaries before consulting you. Check the answers as a class.

Expansion/Homework

(1) If class time is limited, you may want to assign this exercise as homework and then use class time to check answers and work on pronunciation. (2) You may want to have students choose one letter and write three vocabulary words beginning with that letter. In pairs of their own choosing, students can then conduct *Star Daily* interviews on birth order. Students can take on the character of the person in the letter and try to use the three words they have chosen as they answer the reporter's questions.

✪ EXERCISE 2

Focus

To practice the idiomatic vocabulary in this unit; to use the vocabulary in a conversation about birth order theory; to get students to relate their own life experiences and observations to birth order theory.

Setup

Give students a few minutes of preparation time to take notes before they ask and answer the questions using the vocabulary listed. To take advantage of the conversational tone of this exercise, remind students to make lots of eye contact with each other and to refer only to their notes, not to the book. Circulate to listen and to correct errors.

Expansion/Homework

You could invite students to write a brief statement about their birth order and how they think it has affected their personality—perhaps using the first, second, and fourth letters in Exercise 1 as models. This written assignment can be submitted directly to you. Or students may compose this statement in their audio journals.

✪ EXERCISE 3

Focus

To reinforce unit vocabulary by classifying personality traits.

Setup

Have students read aloud the vocabulary listed. Have students work in pairs (with students from different language backgrounds, if possible) to categorize the vocabulary. Encourage them to consult each other and their dictionaries before consulting you. Go over the answers as a class, with students reading their answers aloud to discuss classification and check pronunciation.

Expansion/Homework

If class time is limited, you may want to assign this exercise as homework and use class time to check answers and work on pronunciation.

✪ EXERCISE 4

Focus

To use the unit vocabulary in a free-speaking exercise.

Setup

Have students review the vocabulary in Exercise 3. Have students work in pairs of their own choosing to describe themselves.

Expansion/Homework

You could also have students write a description of a close friend or family member that uses as many of these words as possible. Have students bring in a photograph to show while they read their descriptions aloud in small groups.

✪ EXERCISE 5

Focus

To reinforce unit vocabulary; to apply vocabulary in this unit to a new context: discussions about the personality characteristics best suited for certain roles.

Setup

Have students form small groups to discuss the four scenarios. Remind students to make a choice and stay with it, even though it is not a perfect solution. Encourage students to defend their choices and have fun.

Expansion/Homework

As a follow-up to this exercise, you may want students to select among the words in question 3 to describe their ideal choice of person for the situations in questions 1–4.

 For extra vocabulary practice, have students work on the self-grading vocabulary activities for the unit on the NorthStar Companion Website at **http://www.longman.com/northstar**.

4 Focus on Speaking, PAGE 62

✪✪ A PRONUNCIATION: Grouping Words Together

Suggested Time: 25 minutes 🔊

Focus
To practice listening for and using thought groups in speech.

Setup
Read the introductory passage aloud or have students read silently. Instead of playing the audio, you may want to demonstrate the examples yourself. For Exercise 1, have the class listen to the sentences and then underline the thought groups. Have students work in pairs (with students from different language backgrounds, if possible) to practice pronouncing these sentences. For Exercise 2, have students read the sentences before listening. You could even have them underline the thought groups in each sentence before listening. Play the audio and have students identify the correct sentences. If disagreements arise, replay the segment rather than give the answer. Have students return to their partners to practice pronouncing and identifying the correct sentences.

Expansion/Homework
Have students listen to the first interview as they read along with the transcript. Have them underline the thought groups they hear and then compare their markings in pairs.

✪✪ B GRAMMAR: Adjective Clauses—Identifying and Nonidentifying

Suggested Time: 25 minutes 🔊

Focus
To practice using identifying and nonidentifying adjective clauses in spoken contexts; to review the information and vocabulary used in this unit.

Setup
Have students of different fluency levels work in pairs to examine the sentences and answer the two questions that follow. Ask students to read the grammar explanations silently. Have them work on Exercise 2 individually. Go over the answers as a class. Respond to any questions before pairing up students to do Exercise 3. Model the first one so that students understand that Student A presents the question and that Student B must cover Column A and read only the prompt in Column B. When students finish the first part, have them switch roles.

Expansion/Homework
(1) Exercise 2 works well for homework. Students can complete the exercise at home and then go over the answers in class. (2) For further practice, offer exercises from *Focus on Grammar, Advanced* and from Azar's *Understanding and Using English Grammar*. See the Grammar Book References on page 247 of the Student Book.

✪✪✪ C **STYLE: Starting a Conversation and Keeping It Going**

Suggested Time: 25 minutes

Focus

To get students to practice small talk and specific strategies for keeping a conversation going.

Setup

Ask students to read the opening passage and the list of expressions. Pair stronger and weaker students together to practice applying the expressions in the role plays. Encourage them to dramatize their exchanges; have them stand up, if appropriate, during the role play and use gestures and eye contact to "ham it up."

Expansion/Homework

(1) You may want students to create other situations to role play. (2) If possible, have students record these exchanges and then listen to hear their own performances. You can listen for pronunciation and usage errors, which you can write down and have students correct. (3) Or circulate around the room, listening to conversations. Note any errors on a divided page: Usage/Pronunciation. Have students correct errors and review pronunciation. If one sound is difficult for several students, you may want to give a short lesson on it.

 For extra listening practice, have students use the NorthStar Companion Video.

✪✪✪ D **SPEAKING TOPICS**

Focus

To integrate the concepts, vocabulary, pronunciation skills (grouping words together), grammar (adjective clauses), and style focus (keeping a conversation going) of the unit by listening to and interpreting a song written by a celebrity who suffers from shyness; to role play an interview between a psychologist and the shy celebrity.

Setup

Play the song once with books closed. Play the song again as students listen and complete the lyrics in Exercise 1. Have students individually answer the questions in Exercise 2. Go over the answers as a class. If there is disagreement, welcome it. Encourage students to return to the lyrics to support their points of view. Pair students of varying ages to discuss the questions in Exercise 3. As a class, read the roles and scripts described in Exercise 4. Pair stronger and weaker students together to conduct their interviews. Allow them 20 minutes or even overnight to study their character information, take notes, and develop their interview questions before they begin the role play. Encourage the use of eye contact and gestures to enliven the interaction. Have the partners switch roles in the second role play.

Expansion/Homework

(1) If possible, have students record their role plays and then listen to hear their own performances. They can listen for pronunciation and usage errors, which they can write down and then correct. (2) If taping is not possible, circulate around the room, listening to the role plays. Note any errors on a divided page for each student: Usage/Pronunciation. Have students correct the usage errors and mark the pronunciation words with stress marks over the stressed syllables. Circulate around the room, answering students' questions. As a class, you can review the pronunciation of some of the most frequent errors.

✪E RESEARCH TOPICS

Focus

To practice research and reporting skills by investigating the nature and treatment of a phobia.

Setup

Have students work in pairs of their own choosing to select a phobia to research, locate sources of information through libraries and the Internet, conduct the research, organize the information, and present it to the class in a short (two- or three-minute) presentation.

Expansion/Homework

(1) To provide students with feedback, you may want to videotape or audiorecord these presentations. Students can then listen to their role play and identify errors to correct. (2) If you live in an English-speaking community and you or the students know a person who has struggled with a phobia, invite the person to speak to the class about the phobia and its treatment. Each student can write at least one question to pose to the guest. You may want to review the questions as a class to eliminate redundancy. (3) Have students take notes and write a summary of one report they listened to, using the three-item outline suggested here. (4) For further reading on this topic, the following texts are recommended: *Shyness: What It Is, What to Do about It*, by Philip Zimbardo; *Talking with Confidence for the Painfully Shy*, by Don Gabor; *Shyness: A Bold New Approach: Managing Your Shyness at Work* as well as *Making Small Talk, Navigating Social Situations*, and *Parenting a Shy Child*, all by Bernardo J. Carducci, Ph.D.

Link to NorthStar: Reading and Writing

If time allows, you could do a writing topic from Section 4C (at home) and a speaking topic (in class). You will probably want to choose the research topic, that fits your students and the environment best. When students speak, remind them to use examples and vocabulary from the Reading/Writing unit on optimism, self-confidence, and the pursuit of success.

The Tipping Point

OVERVIEW

Theme:	Trends
Listenings:	Listening One: *The Tipping Point* 　　An interview with the author Listening Two: *Tipping Points in Fighting Crime* 　　More excerpts from the interview
Critical Thinking Skills:	Interpret graphs Identify influences on personal behavior Analyze case study Critique an interviewer's strategy Correlate personal observations to the Tipping Point Theory Critique the Broken Window Theory Define problems and propose solutions
Listening Tasks:	Interview a classmate and write down the responses Summarize main points Listen for details Interpret a speaker's attitude Relate listenings to personal experiences Identify stress patterns Listen to and comment on a public service announcement Take notes in outline form Research a successful product at a local company
Speaking Tasks:	Make predictions Express and defend opinions Simulate a neighborhood advisory committee meeting Act out a scripted interview Use metaphors to make a point Use introductory expressions to extemporaneously restate information Develop and present a public service announcement Collaborate on a plan to change a trend Present research findings on a successful product
Pronunciation:	Stress changing suffixes
Vocabulary:	Context clues Word definitions Synonyms Metaphors
Grammar:	Adverbs clauses of result

UNIT SUMMARY

This unit explores a social behavior theory put forth by Malcolm Caldwell in his book *The Tipping Point: How Little Things Can Make a Big Difference*. In the first interview, Caldwell identifies three types of people who are key to the rapid dissemination of an idea. In the second interview, Caldwell describes how small changes in the environment of New York City subways spurred a dramatic drop in crime.

The companion unit in *NorthStar: Reading and Writing* explores how the book *Silent Spring* by Rachel Carson galvanized the popular environmental movement.

1 Focus on the Topic, PAGE 73

✪✪✪A PREDICTING

Suggested Time: 10 minutes ⏱

Focus
To predict the content of the unit based on the title, the graph, and students' knowledge of trends.

Setup
Ask students to read the title and look at the graphs. To check graph comprehension ask, *How many murders were there in New York City in 1992? How about in 1997? How many fax machines were sold in 1984? How about in 1987? How about in 1989?* Point out that the graphs illustrate sudden change. Then have students read the questions. You may need to give students the definition of *tip* (verb) or have students look up the word in their dictionaries. Have students share their responses in small groups.

Expansion/Homework
You may want to lead a follow-up discussion to help the whole class explore the possibilities of how such behavior changed so suddenly. Encourage a range of responses by writing all students' ideas on the board.

✪✪B SHARING INFORMATION

Suggested Time: 15 minutes ⏱

Focus
To encourage students to reflect on what factors influence their own behavior.

Setup
Read the opening paragraph aloud to the class. Briefly discuss possible answers to the question and then explain that students are going to use interviews to examine which factors influence changes in their own behavior. Pair students of varying

ages and backgrounds to conduct the interviews. Invite the pairs to report their findings to the class. Tally up which factors most influence student behavior.

✪✪✪ C   PREPARING TO LISTEN

BACKGROUND
Suggested Time: 15 minutes 🕐

Focus
To give students an example of sudden social change; to awaken interest in and aid student comprehension of the listening that follows.

Setup
Have students read the passage individually. Check comprehension by asking, *What is tetanus? How did the health center try at first to inform students about the dangers of tetanus? Did their campaign work? Why did they start a contest? What was the contest prize?* For Exercise 1, have students from different language backgrounds form small groups to design their own inoculation campaign and present their ideas to the class. For Exercise 2, have students individually read the solution on page 242. Check their comprehension and ask, *How was this information different from the information the health center distributed earlier?* Have students return to their groups to discuss why the solution was so effective. You may want to lead a follow-up discussion, reviewing the most interesting points in each group's discussion.

Expansion/Homework
You could convert the reading portions of these activities into listening exercises by reading the introductory and solution text aloud as students listen. Check their comprehension by asking the questions listed in Setup.

VOCABULARY FOR COMPREHENSION
Suggested Time: 15 minutes 🕐

Focus
To acquaint students with concepts and vocabulary in the listening that follows.

Setup
As a class, review the pronunciation of the underlined words in Exercise 1. Then have students complete the exercise individually and compare answers with a partner (someone from a different language background, if possible). Encourage students to consult each other and their dictionaries before consulting you. For Exercise 2, pair students of similar levels to match the definitions and words.

Expansion/Homework
(1) You may want to assign both exercises as homework and then use class time to check answers and correct pronunciation. (2) If students struggle to guess the meaning of the underlined words in Exercise 1, refer them to the list of definitions in Exercise 2. (3) To help students memorize vocabulary, have them work in pairs to quiz each other on the definitions in Exercise 2. One can act as the teacher; the other can play the student. Then have them switch roles.

2 Focus on Listening, PAGE 78

✪✪✪ A   LISTENING ONE: *The Tipping Point*

Suggested Time: 10 minutes ⏱

Focus

To present an interview with Malcolm Gladwell, author of the book *The Tipping Point*; to encourage students to predict the content of the interview.

Setup

Give students a few minutes to read the opening paragraphs. Have students pair up with a neighboring classmate to define *a connector*. Play the excerpt and have students check their predictions.

Expansion/Homework

You may prefer to convert this into a listening activity by reading the opening paragraphs aloud, as students listen with their books closed.

✪✪✪ LISTENING FOR MAIN IDEAS

Suggested Time: 20 minutes ⏱

Focus

To help students identify the main ideas in the interview.

Setup

Ask students to read the prompts before listening. Play the interview and then have students write their definitions. Have students compare their ideas with a neighboring classmate. If disagreements arise, play the interview as many times as needed for students to write satisfactory definitions.

Expansion/Homework

You may want to explicitly connect the notion of a "tipping point" with the discussion of important communicators, such as connectors, mavens, and salesmen. Ask students, *How do connectors, mavens, and salesmen influence people's behavior? How do these special people create new trends?*

LISTENING FOR DETAILS

Suggested Time: 10 minutes ⏱

Focus

To get students to listen carefully again, this time for specific pieces of information.

Setup

First have students read the true/false statements, writing in answers they already know. Play the interview again. Have students complete their responses and then compare their answers with a neighboring classmate. If disagreements arise, replay the interview rather than give the answer.

Expansion/Homework

You could ask each student to write an additional true/false statement to present to the class.

✪✪ REACTING TO THE LISTENING
Suggested Time: 25 minutes

Focus

To encourage students to interpret tone of voice and word choice to determine a speaker's attitude; to promote critical discussion of and reflection on the interview.

Setup

For each excerpt in Exercise 1, have students listen, answer the questions, and then discuss their answers in small groups (with students from different language backgrounds, if possible). For Exercise 2, have students stay in their same small groups to discuss the questions. You may want to define the word *trend* before students read the questions.

Expansion/Homework

Have one student from each group report one interesting idea that emerged in the group discussion to the class.

✪✪✪ B LISTENING TWO: *Tipping Points in Fighting Crime*
Suggested Time: 20 minutes

Focus

To relate small changes in subway management to the sudden decrease in subway crime in New York City in the 1990s, according to the theories presented in the book *The Tipping Point*; to listen to another interview with Malcolm Gladwell.

Setup

Ask students to read the incomplete sentences in Exercise 1 before listening to the interview. As students listen, they can complete the sentences. Have students compare their answers with a neighboring classmate or with the whole class. Have students of varying ages and experiences form small groups to discuss the questions in Exercise 2.

Expansion/Homework

(1) Circulate around the room, listening as students discuss Exercise 2. Note any errors, using a divided page: Usage/Pronunciation. Have students correct the usage errors and mark the pronunciation words with stress marks over the stressed syllables. As a class, you can review the pronunciation of some of the most frequent errors. (2) After their in-class discussions, students can compose their final responses to the questions in Exercise 2 and record them in their audio journals. (3) If students are reticent, list examples of social problems on the board (drug addiction, teenage motherhood, domestic violence) and as a class discuss how to craft a response plan for each problem using the *tipping point* theoretical framework.

✪✪✪ C LINKING LISTENINGS ONE AND TWO

Suggested Time: 25 minutes 🕐

Focus
To apply behavior theory presented in the book *The Tipping Point* in solving neighborhood problems; to perform a class role play to practice the concepts and language presented in this unit.

Setup
Read the introductory information about the troubled neighborhood with the class. Have students of varying ages and experiences form groups of three to prepare a "clean-up" plan. Set a time limit of 20 minutes for their discussion. Circulate around the room, offering direction and encouragement. Remind students that the proposed changes must be consistent with the two theories: *Power of Context* and *Law of the Few*. Invite the groups to present their plans. Encourage the audience to ask questions about each plan.

Expansion/Homework
(1) To promote active use of new words, you may want to list vocabulary from Section 1C (Vocabulary for Comprehension) on the board. If students are using the companion text, *NorthStar: Reading and Writing*, you may also want to include vocabulary from that unit's Section 1C on the board. Or you could create a list integrating the vocabulary from the Listening/Speaking and Reading/Writing strands. See the Word List for each unit at the end of the Teacher's Manual and on the Companion Website at **http://www.longman.com/northstar**. (2) After their presentations, students could incorporate the feedback they receive from the class and write a final "clean-up" plan to record in their audio journal. (3) Encourage your students to follow this topic in the news or online. Have them bring any articles they find that mention tipping points to class.

Link to *NorthStar: Reading and Writing*
Students using the companion text can include the third factor in popularizing an idea, the "stickiness factor," in their clean-up plans.

2 Focus on Vocabulary, PAGE 84

✪ EXERCISES 1 AND 2
Suggested Time: 15 minutes 🕐

Focus
To introduce the concept of literal and metaphoric meaning; to use metaphors to write about concepts introduced in this unit.

Setup
For Exercise 1, read the introductory information to the class and review the pronunciation of the expressions. Divide the class into small groups of students from varying language backgrounds. Have the groups sort the expressions into

the two categories. Review their choices as a class. In the same groups, have students complete the sentences in Exercise 2. In class, review several examples of student sentences for each expression.

Expansion/Homework

In pairs, have students explain the change in criminal behavior on New York City subways using at least five of these metaphors.

Link to *NorthStar: Reading and Writing*

You could have students use several of these metaphors to explain how the book *Silent Spring* spurred the environmental movement.

✪ EXERCISE 3
Suggested Time: 10 minutes ⏱

Focus

To apply unit vocabulary to a new context: an interview between two specialists in the development and spread of new ideas and products.

Setup

Have students read through the whole interview before writing their answers. Review the pronunciation of the listed vocabulary before dividing students into pairs to role play the interview.

Expansion/Homework

(1) If class time is limited, you may want to assign this exercise as homework and use class time to role play the interviews. (2) Using the pronunciation skills they learned in Unit 3, students could silently read through the completed interview and mark the thought groups before they read their roles aloud.

For extra vocabulary practice, have students work on the self-grading vocabulary activities for the unit on the NorthStar Companion Website at **http://www.longman.com/northstar**.

◢**4** Focus on Speaking, PAGE 89

✪✪ A PRONUNCIATION: Stress Changing Suffixes
Suggested Time: 25 minutes 🕐

Focus

To identify the shift in stress patterns when suffixes are added to root words; to anticipate in speech the stress of words with suffixes; to expand students' vocabulary by deriving variations in word forms.

Setup

Read the introductory passage aloud or have students read silently. Instead of playing the audio, you may want to demonstrate the examples yourself. For Exercises 1 and 2, have students repeat the words and then mark the stressed syllables. Have students compare their markings with a neighboring classmate or write the correct markings on the board after each word is pronounced. For Exercise 2, pair students from different language backgrounds to do the activity. If disagreements arise, refer students to another student model instead of giving the answer yourself.

Expansion/Homework

Some students can grasp stress better if it is accompanied with a gesture; the physical movement focuses attention on the cadence of the word. You can have students swing their hands, shift their weight, or stomp their feet to reflect the stressed syllable of a word.

✪✪B GRAMMAR: Adverb Clauses of Result

Suggested Time: 25 minutes 🕙

Focus

To introduce students to adverb clauses of result; to have students practice these clauses in writing and speaking as they review concepts introduced in this unit.

Setup

Have students of different fluency levels work in pairs to examine the sentences and answer the two questions that follow. Ask students to read the grammar explanations silently. Have them work on Exercise 2 individually and then compare answers with a neighboring classmate. Check comprehension of the story by asking, *Who was Paul Revere? Who was William Dawes? Why was Paul Revere's ride so successful? Why wasn't William Dawes's ride successful?* Pair students of similar fluency levels to do Exercise 3.

Expansion/Homework

(1) Exercise 2 works well for homework. Students can complete the exercise at home and then go over the answers in class to work on pronunciation and discuss the story. (2) For further practice, offer exercises from *Focus on Grammar, Advanced* and from Azar's *Understanding and Using English Grammar.* See the Grammar Book References on page 247 of the Student Book.

✪✪✪C STYLE: Making a Point with Metaphors

Suggested Time: 25 minutes 🕙

Focus

To get students to practice using metaphors when making a point.

Setup

Ask students to read the introductory information, directions, and list of expressions. Model the example with another student. Pair students of similar fluency levels to practice applying the expressions while reiterating information presented in this unit. You may want to write the expressions on the board so that students don't refer to their books. Encourage them to make eye contact. Circulate among the pairs, listening and correcting.

Expansion/Homework

(1) If possible, have students record these exchanges and then listen to their own performances. They can listen for pronunciation and usage errors, which they may then correct. (2) For a written assignment, students can restate all four prompts using appropriate metaphors.

 For extra listening practice, have students use the NorthStar Companion Video.

✪✪✪ D   SPEAKING TOPIC

Focus

To integrate the concepts, vocabulary, pronunciation skills (stress changing suffixes), grammar (adverb clauses of result), and style focus (making a point with metaphors) of the unit in the development of public service announcements.

Setup

Ask students to read the introductory information about "sticky" messages and PSAs. For Exercise 1, have students close their eyes as they listen to the PSA. For Exercise 2, play the PSA again, as students fill in the outline. You may need to play the PSA several times for students to complete their outlines. For Exercise 3, have students of similar backgrounds and interests work together to develop their own PSAs. If recording equipment is not available, have student perform their PSAs for the class.

Expansion/Homework

As students present their PSAs, note pronunciation and usage errors. At the end of the presentations, present your notes—either for the class or for each group—and have students correct the errors. Help students work on pronunciation.

Link to *NorthStar: Reading and Writing*

Students could also develop a PSA with one of the messages in Rachel Carson's book *Silent Spring*.

✪ E   RESEARCH TOPICS

Focus

To develop a plan to create a new trend using the theories presented in this unit; to explore how local companies have successfully marketed a product.

Setup

Have students form groups of their own choosing. As the groups are developing their strategies, circulate around the classroom, giving feedback and support. Bring paper and markers to class to encourage students to use visual aids in their class presentations. For the interviews, you may want to suggest specific local businesses that have successfully launched new products. Students can summarize their interviews and present them to the class.

Expansion/Homework

For further reading on this topic, the following texts are recommended: *The Tipping Point: How Little Things Can Make a Big Difference*, by Malcolm Gladwell; and *Unleashing the Ideavirus*, by Seth Godin and Malcolm Gladwell.

Link to *NorthStar: Reading and Writing*

If time allows, you could do a speaking topic from Section 4D (in class) and a writing topic (at home). You will probably want to choose the research topic that fits your students and the classroom environment best. When students speak, remind them to use examples and vocabulary from the Reading/Writing material on the environmental movement.

Feng Shui: Ancient Wisdom Travels West

OVERVIEW	
Theme:	Cross-Cultural Insights

Listenings:	Listening One: *Interview with a Feng Shui Expert*
	    A conversation with Kirsten Lagatree
	Listening Two: *Feng Shui in the Newsroom*
	    The expert redesigns a space

Critical Thinking Skills:	Interpret quotations Evaluate environments according to the principles of feng shui Support opinions with information from the text Distinguish between common sense and superstition Infer word meaning from context Plan a space conforming to feng shui principles Develop a logical argument for and against an issue
Listening Tasks:	Explain main ideas Listen to classmate summaries to complete a chart Identify supporting details Interpret speaker's attitude and tone Relate listening to personal environment Take notes using a graphic organizer Synthesize information from two listenings Identify patterns of stress reduction in speech
Speaking Tasks:	Summarize information in an information gap activity Express and defend opinions Act out a scripted interview Use new vocabulary and discourse connectors in extemporaneous responses Use functional language to emphasize a point Role play a meeting Conduct an interview and report results Report research findings on phony cross-cultural products
Pronunciation:	Reductions with the auxiliary *have*
Vocabulary:	Word definitions Synonyms Context clues Word forms
Grammar:	Spoken discourse connectors

UNIT SUMMARY

This unit deals with the Western approach to feng shui, the ancient Asian practice of designing architectural spaces to create physical and psychological comfort. Listening One is an interview with a journalist who writes on feng shui. She describes how feng shui is practiced and how it can influence people's daily lives. Listening Two is another excerpt from the same interview, focusing on how to rearrange actual office space to maximize positive feng shui.

The companion unit in *NorthStar: Reading and Writing* explores the impact of immigration on families.

1 Focus on the Topic, PAGE 99

✪✪✪A PREDICTING

Suggested Time: 5 minutes

Focus
To get students to predict the meaning of feng shui from the context of the cartoon.

Setup
Ask students to read the title, look at the cartoon, and discuss the questions with a neighboring classmate.

Expansion/Homework
As a class, you may want to elicit responses and write them on the board.

✪✪B SHARING INFORMATION

Suggested Time: 20 minutes

Focus
To develop students' awareness of the importance of place; to get students to discuss freely their experiences and thoughts about the relationship between people and place.

Setup
Have students from different cultural backgrounds form small groups to discuss the questions. Some of the language in the quotation may be challenging. Encourage students to consult each other and their dictionaries before consulting you. Have students tell the class any interesting insights they heard in their group discussions.

Expansion/Homework
(1) You may want to read the quotations aloud as students listen with books closed. Discuss the questions as a class. (2) To bring the material to a more immediate level, ask the students to analyze the classroom environment by asking, *How does this classroom enhance or detract from your learning*

experience? How do the seating arrangement, lighting, noise level, and size of the room affect how you work together and learn in this room? (3) Encourage your students to follow this topic in the news or online. Have them bring to class any articles they find that mention feng shui.

✪✪✪ C PREPARING TO LISTEN

BACKGROUND
Suggested Time: 30 minutes

Focus
To introduce students to the concept of feng shui; to practice summarizing skills; to awaken interest in and aid comprehension of the listening that follows.

Setup
Divide the class into groups of five students. Within each group, assign a paragraph to each student. Set a time limit of seven minutes for students to read and take notes on their assigned paragraph. After all members of the groups have explained their part of reading, check comprehension by asking, *What does feng shui mean? What is the theory of feng shui? What is ch'i? What is the origin of feng shui? Why has feng shui spread to the West?* Then have students from different cultural backgrounds work together in pairs to rate the items in the chart. Encourage students to state the reasons they rate items favorably or unfavorably. After students have discussed the chart thoroughly, ask for any reactions to the answers.

Expansion/Homework
(1) If classroom time is limited, you may want to assign the entire reading as homework and then review comprehension in class. (2) You could convert this into a listening exercise by reading the text aloud as students listen. Check their comprehension with the questions listed in Setup.

VOCABULARY FOR COMPREHENSION
Suggested Time: 15 minutes

Focus
To acquaint students with vocabulary that is often used when describing feng shui; to aid listening comprehension.

Setup
As a class, practice pronouncing the underlined words. Ask students to work individually to complete sentences. Go over the answers as a class, with students reading them aloud so you can correct pronunciation.

Expansion/Homework
(1) If classroom time is limited, you may want to assign the section as homework and use class time to check answers and work on pronunciation. (2) To help students memorize vocabulary, have them work in pairs to quiz each other on the definitions. One can play the teacher; the other can play the student. Then have them switch roles.

② Focus on Listening, PAGE 104

✪✪✪ A   LISTENING ONE: *Interview with a Feng Shui Expert*

Suggested Time: 10 minutes ⏱

Focus
To get students to predict the positive impact favorable feng shui can have on a person; to help students predict the content of the interview.

Setup
Have students work with a partner to predict how favorable feng shui could make a person feel. To encourage use of the vocabulary learned in Section 1C, write the words on the board for students' reference. Have students listen to the excerpt and compare that list with their own. Ask students to share any reactions with the class.

Expansion/Homework
As a class, you may want to elicit ideas and write them on the board for students' reference after listening to the excerpt.

✪✪✪ LISTENING FOR MAIN IDEAS

Suggested Time: 15 minutes ⏱

Focus
To help students listen for the main ideas in an extended interview about one journalist's experience with feng shui.

Setup
Have students read the chart before listening. Play the interview as students write their notes. Then have students compare their notes with a neighboring classmate. You may also want to call on individual students to restate the key information for each point. You might need to play the interview more than once for students to grasp all the key points.

Expansion/Homework
Before you begin the listening you may want explain that Donald Trump is one of the richest and most successful real estate developers in the United States.

✪✪✪ LISTENING FOR DETAILS

Suggested Time: 20 minutes ⏱

Focus
To get students to listen carefully again, this time for specific pieces of information.

Setup
First have students read the questions, answering any they can. Play the interview again, letting students compare answers after each part. If disagreements arise, replay the segment rather than give the answer. In some cases, students may even want to listen a third time.

Expansion/Homework

(1) You could have pairs of students quiz each other by reading the questions aloud. Student A can read the questions in Part One to Student B. For Part Two, they can switch roles. To aid in their exchanges, you may want to write phrases for expressing uncertainty on the board (*I guess . . . /Perhaps . . . /I have no idea. . !/ Beats me*). (2) To help strengthen students' overall grasp of the material, you may want to have students orally restate the listening in pairs, using the key words in Section 1C as a guide.

✪✪ REACTING TO THE LISTENING
Suggested Time: 25 minutes 🕐

Focus

To encourage students to interpret tone of voice and word choice to determine a speaker's attitude; to encourage students to consider several possibilities in their responses.

Setup

Have students read the prompts before they listen to the excerpts. Allow students a few minutes to think about their responses before discussing them in small groups. If there is disagreement, welcome it. Encourage students to support their points of view with details from the interview. Emphasize that it is possible for students to have varying opinions, as long as their reasoning is sound. To enrich this discussion, try to pair students of varying backgrounds and ages. Have the pairs report any especially interesting or insightful ideas they discussed to the class.

Expansion/Homework

To teach students to infer meaning and look for a range of answers, you may want to do one excerpt as a class before playing the others. Encourage a range of responses by writing all students' ideas on the board. Emphasize that it is possible for students to have varying inferences as long as their reasoning is sound.

Link to *NorthStar: Reading and Writing*

In the companion unit, Eva Hoffman and Elizabeth Wong describe feeling "lost in translation" as they adapted to their new cultures. Ask, *Do ideas and trends, as well as people, get lost in translation as they are adapted to new cultures? If so, how?* Encourage students to illustrate their points with concrete examples from their own cultures.

✪✪✪ B   LISTENING TWO: *Feng Shui in the Newsroom*
Suggested Time: 30 minutes 🕐

Focus

To deepen students' understanding of feng shui; to give students a concrete example of feng shui by analyzing the layout of a newsroom with a Western student of feng shui.

Setup

Have students look at the chart carefully before listening to the audio. After each listening, pause to let students compare answers. As they listen, have them fill in the chart. Some information on the audio is not addressed in the chart.

Expansion/Homework

Students can write that extra information on a separate piece of paper to compare with a neighboring classmate. Encourage students to enjoy this exercise.

✪✪✪ C ▐ LINKING LISTENINGS ONE AND TWO

Suggested Time: 25 minutes

Focus

To get students to remember and synthesize information from the interviews; to practice applying the principles of feng shui to a space students use daily.

Setup

Have students work individually to analyze and redecorate a space using feng shui. When presenting their ideas, have students use a large sheet of paper divided into two sections: one for the current layout and one for the new layout with favorable feng shui. Keep the presentations to five minutes each.

Expansion/Homework

(1) You may want students to work in groups to develop new layouts for the classroom. Have each group present its ideas with the guidelines mentioned in Setup. The class can then vote on which layout would bring the most favorable feng shui. If possible, try rearranging the classroom according to the best layout, and, after a few weeks, ask students to comment on whether it has influenced them. (2) As students present their plans, note pronunciation and usage errors. At the end of the presentations, present your notes—either for the class or for each group—and have students correct the errors. Help students work on pronunciation.

❸ Focus on Vocabulary, PAGE 109

✪ EXERCISE 1
Suggested Time: 25 minutes

Focus

To give more practice with the idiomatic vocabulary in this unit; to add fun and interest to the topic with a fictitious interview between a feng shui master and the real-estate tycoon Donald Trump.

Setup

As a class, practice pronouncing the list of words. Then have students work with a partner (someone from a different language background, if possible) to read aloud and complete the interview. To encourage interaction in this exercise, have students read the information in the book silently and then look at their partners to speak. For the vocabulary, encourage them to consult each other and their dictionaries before consulting you. Check the answers as a class.

Expansion/Homework

(1) If class time is limited, you may want to assign this as homework and use class time for students to read the interview dramatically and work on pronunciation. (2) Using the pronunciation skills they learned in Unit 3, students could silently read through the completed conversation and mark the thought groups before they read their roles aloud. (3) To encourage further practice of the vocabulary in this unit, you may want to assign students to write a paragraph that uses as many of the expressions as possible. For fun, they could imagine a letter to Lagatree or Trump and write it as a class.

✪ EXERCISE 2
Suggested Time: 15 minutes 🕐

Focus

To practice the idiomatic vocabulary presented in this unit in a guided conversation about feng shui.

Setup

Give students a few minutes of preparation time to take notes before they use the vocabulary listed to ask and answer the questions. To promote the conversational tone of this exercise, remind students to make lots of eye contact and to speak only when looking at their partners.

 For extra vocabulary practice, have students work on the self-grading vocabulary activities for the unit on the NorthStar Companion Website at **http://www.longman.com/northstar**.

4 Focus on Speaking, PAGE 112

✪✪ A   PRONUNCIATION: Reductions with the Auxiliary *have*
Suggested Time: 25 minutes 🕐

Focus

To raise awareness of and practice pronunciation of modal perfect forms in a spoken context: a true story of how a Kung Fu master ignored the influence of feng shui and then encountered disaster.

Setup

Read the introductory passage aloud or have students read it silently. Instead of playing the audio, you may want to demonstrate the examples yourself. For Exercise 1, tell students to read the whole story before playing it. Play the story, while students fill in the verbs. Play the story again, while students draw stress marks (´) over the stressed words. Go over the answers as a class, with students reading their answers aloud to check pronunciation. For Exercise 2, have pairs of students from different language backgrounds practice the exchanges. To encourage the conversational tone of this exercise, have students read the information in the book silently and then look at their partners to speak. They may need to break the information into smaller pieces to retell it. It doesn't matter how frequently they refer to the book as long as they are looking at their partner when they speak.

Expansion/Homework

(1) Using the pronunciation skills they learned in Unit 3, students could silently read the completed story and mark the thought groups before they read it aloud. (2) You could have students do dramatic readings of the story of the Kung Fu master. Encourage them to enhance their reading with background music and sound effects. (3) You may want to conduct a class discussion about students' experiences with bad luck. Ask them, *Have you ever had a bad event foretold by a practice like feng shui (tarot cards, astrology, hexagrams)? Did you try to prevent it? What happened?*

✪✪ B GRAMMAR: Spoken Discourse Connectors

Suggested Time: 25 minutes 🕐

Focus

To practice spoken discourse connectors; to review the information and vocabulary used in this unit.

Setup

Have students of different fluency levels work in pairs to examine the excerpt from Listening One and answer the two questions that follow. Ask students to read the grammar explanations silently. Have them work on Exercise 2 in pairs. Then have students compare answers with those of a neighboring pair. For Exercise 3, have students work in pairs and take turns responding to the statements with the appropriate discourse connectors.

Expansion/Homework

(1) Exercises 1 and 2 work well for homework. Students can go over the answers in class to work on pronunciation. (2) You may want to ask students to choose one topic in Exercise 3 to present to the class in a short two-minute talk. Have students use at least three connectors in their talks. As the class listens, have them write the connectors they hear. (3) For further practice, offer exercises from *Focus on Grammar, Advanced* and from Azar's *Understanding and Using English Grammar*. See the Grammar Book References on page 247 of the Student Book.

✪✪✪ C STYLE: Emphasizing a Point

Suggested Time: 25 minutes 🕐

Focus

To raise awareness of the way speakers emphasize their points; to get students to practice informal expressions for emphasizing a point as they discuss feng shui.

Setup

Ask students to read the introductory passage and then read the examples as they listen. Have students practice saying the phrases with affect before they read the chart on page 116. Pair students of similar fluency levels to do Exercise 2. Allow them a few minutes to read through the prompts before they begin. Encourage use of eye contact and gestures to enhance the emphatic tone of these exchanges.

Expansion/Homework

(1) If possible, have students record the exchanges in Exercise 2 and then listen to their own performances. They can listen for pronunciation and usage errors, which they can write down and then correct. (2) If recording is not possible, circulate around the room, listening as students speak. Note any errors, using a divided page: Usage/Pronunciation. Have students correct the usage errors and mark the pronunciation words with stress marks over the stressed syllables. Circulate around the room, answering students' questions. As a class, you can review the pronunciation of some of the most frequent errors. (3) Have each pair stand up in front of the class and deliver a dramatic exchange modeled on one of the items in Exercise 2. Be sure they use stress, intonation, and gestures to strengthen their emphasis.

 For extra listening practice, have students use the NorthStar Companion Video.

✪✪✪ D SPEAKING TOPIC

Focus

To integrate the concepts, vocabulary, pronunciation skills (reductions with the auxiliary *have*), grammar (spoken discourse connectors), and style focus (emphasizing a point) of the unit; to explore further the cultural and political implications of feng shui in a fun context: decorating the White House.

Setup

Ask students to read the fictional article. Check comprehension and ask, *How is life in the White House these days? What is the President's solution? For the President, what does the White House symbolize? How does the First Lady feel about the President's proposal? For the First Lady, what does the White House symbolize?* Divide the class into two groups. Have each group read the directions and outline its arguments, referring to the transcripts and notes for any supporting information. You can be the meeting chairperson. Invite each group to present its position and then let them discuss the strengths and weakness of each other's arguments. Work toward a solution. For homework, have students write their personal opinions in a paragraph that they can submit to you for evaluation.

Expansion/Homework
(1) You could convert the reading portion of these activities into a listening exercise by reading the article to the class and then checking comprehension with the questions listed in Setup. (2) During the role play, take note of the most salient usage and pronunciation errors, and comment on the content and delivery of ideas. You can then distribute these notes to the individual students. Have them return the papers to you with the usage errors corrected and the pronunciation words marked with stress marks over the stressed syllables. As a class, review the pronunciation of the most frequent errors.

✪E   RESEARCH TOPICS

Focus
To explore other Eastern practices that have become popular in the West; to research on the Web products that exploit the popularity of feng shui.

Setup
For the first topic, brainstorm with students strategies for finding interviewees. Have students in pairs of their own choosing write questions they would like to ask. Have students present their findings to the class. For the second topic, have students research individually or in pairs. Have students present their product findings to the class. In a follow-up discussion ask, *Why do you think there are so many products on the market that promise to bring peace and harmony? Do you know of any products that actually do bring peace and harmony? How do these products work?*

Expansion/Homework
(1) For a general discussion, you may also want to ask students, *What traditions and values have traveled to the East from the West? Why do you think these traditions have become popular? How are they practiced differently in the East?* (2) If you live in an English-speaking community and you or the students know a person who is dedicated to an Asian tradition, invite the person to speak to the class. Each student can write at least one question to pose to the guest. You may want to review the questions as a class to eliminate redundancy. (3) For further reading on this topic, the following texts are recommended: *Clear Your Clutter with Feng Shui*, by Karen Kingston; *Feng Shui: Arranging Your Home to Change Your Life*, by Kirsten Lagatree; *Fixer Chao*, by Han Ong; *Feng Shui*, by Angel Thomson; and *Feng Shui*, by Lillian Too.

Link to *NorthStar: Reading and Writing*
If time allows, you could do a speaking topic from Section 4D (in class) and a writing topic (at home). You will probably want to choose the research topic that fits your students and the classroom environment best. When students speak, remind them to use vocabulary and examples from the Reading/Writing material on immigration.

Spiritual Renewal

OVERVIEW	
Theme:	Religion

Listenings:	Listening One: *The Religious Tradition of Fasting*
	    A news report
	Listening Two: *Describing Monastic Life*
	    An interview with an admirer

Critical Thinking Skills:	Interpret quotations Challenge assumptions and stereotypes of monastic life Infer word meaning from context Analyze introductory statements and word usage Classify language Hypothesize rationale for various religious practices Evaluate appeal and benefits of spiritual practices
Listening Tasks:	Restate main ideas Listen for details Identify main ideas Listen and take notes on language usage Relate listening to personal preferences, experiences, and values Identify vowel patterns in speech

Speaking Tasks:	Make predictions
	Brainstorm motivations for spiritual renewal
	Express and defend opinions
	Summarize a reading using new vocabulary
	Use new vocabulary and expressions for hesitation in
	    extemporaneous responses
	Act out a scripted interview
	Plan and tell an anecdote using appropriate words and
	    phrases
	Simulate a community meeting
	Plan and present a five-minute talk on monasticism

Pronunciation:	Vowel alternation
Vocabulary:	Context clues Word definitions Synonyms
Grammar:	Count and non-count nouns and their quantifiers

UNIT SUMMARY

This unit explores the appeal and work of monasteries in contemporary society. Listening One is a report on how different religions understand the benefits of fasting. Listening Two is an interview with William Claassen, a man who has researched monastic communities around the world. Additional readings on Thomas Merton and Tenzin Palmo further explore the lifestyle and work of contemporary monks.

The companion unit in *NorthStar: Reading and Writing* explores the defining role of faith in one's world view and offers a global definition of religion.

1 Focus on the Topic, PAGE 121

✪✪✪ A PREDICTING

Suggested Time: 5 minutes ⏱

Focus
To get students thinking about the appeal of visiting a monastery; to predict the content of the unit based on the title and the photograph.

Setup
Ask students to read the title and questions and look at the photograph. Have students pair up with a neighboring classmate to discuss their responses.

Expansion/Homework
You may want to do this section as a class, eliciting responses and writing them on the board. Students may enjoy returning to their predictions after they learn more about this theme.

✪✪ B SHARING INFORMATION

Suggested Time: 20 minutes 🕐

Focus
To expose students to concepts about spiritual life (faith, heart, quiet, and solitude), which are further explored in this unit; to encourage students to identify their own values and beliefs.

Setup
Divide the class into small groups of students of varying ages and backgrounds. Ask students to take turns reading each quotation aloud and then paraphrasing it. Circulate around the classroom to answer questions and clarify new vocabulary. Follow up with a brief class discussion. Ask, *What quotation did you like best? Why? Were there any quotations you didn't like? Why not?*

Expansion/Homework

This reading can be used as a jigsaw: Photocopy the text and then cut out the quotations. Divide the class into groups of four. Give students a quotation to read and have them take notes. With only notes in hand, have students explain their quotations to their groups.

Link to *NorthStar: Reading and Writing*

Ask, *Which quotations do you think the Dalai Lama would like?*

✪✪✪ C ██ PREPARING TO LISTEN ████████████████████████████

BACKGROUND
Suggested Time: 15 minutes 🕙

Focus

To introduce students to the universal features of monasteries; to challenge students' perceptions of monastic life; to awaken interest in and aid student comprehension of the listening that follows.

Setup

Have students read the introductory paragraph and question. Elicit a few ideas and images from students about monastic life before turning to the next exercise. Have students individually read the next paragraph and read and react to the statements. As students finish, have them pair up with a partner to compare answers and read the explanations on page 242 of the Student Book. During this activity, encourage students to discuss their ideas fully and challenge any assumptions they may have about monks and monasteries.

Expansion/Homework

(1) You can convert this into a listening/speaking exercise. Read the statements orally. Have the class discuss whether they are fact or myth. If students are unable to decide, read aloud the information on page 242 of the Student Book (omitting the answer) and have them decide. (2) Encourage your students to follow this topic in the news or online. Have them bring any articles they find that mention monasteries or monks to class.

VOCABULARY FOR COMPREHENSION
Suggested Time: 15 minutes 🕙

Focus

To acquaint students with vocabulary used when discussing religious life and monastic communities; to aid comprehension of the listening.

Setup

Review the pronunciation of the underlined words embedded in the text. Ask students to read the Web newsletter article individually and match the underlined words with their definitions. Go over the answers as a class, with students reading them aloud so you can correct pronunciation.

Expansion/Homework

(1) If class time is limited, you may want to assign the exercise as homework and use class time to check answers and correct pronunciation. (2) To help students memorize vocabulary, have them work in pairs to quiz each other on the definitions. One can play the teacher; the other can play the student. Then have them switch roles. (3) For homework, students could choose one journal entry to read aloud in their audio journals. This provides students with the opportunity to focus solely on their pronunciation.

2 Focus on Listening, PAGE 125

✪✪✪ A | LISTENING ONE: *The Religious Tradition of Fasting*

Suggested Time: 10 minutes 🕙

Focus

To help students predict the contents of the interview; to present a report about the role of fasting in diverse religions.

Setup

Have students silently read the introduction. Pair students of varying ages and backgrounds to make their predictions. Encourage them to use the vocabulary introduced in the previous section by writing the list of words on the board. Have students listen to the excerpt and then check their predictions.

Expansion/Homework

You may want the whole class to make predictions while you write students' ideas on the board. After listening, students can check the board to see how accurate their predictions were.

✪✪✪ LISTENING FOR MAIN IDEAS

Suggested Time: 20 minutes 🕙

Focus

To help students listen for the main ideas in a radio report on fasting.

Setup

Have students read the information before listening. Play the interview while students complete the exercise. Review students' answers as a class. If there is disagreement, have students listen to the interview again.

Expansion/Homework

To add challenge, convert this into a note-taking activity. As they listen, have students take notes using a divided page: Main Ideas/Details. Then students can open their books and use their notes to complete the exercise.

✪✪✪ **LISTENING FOR DETAILS**
Suggested Time: 20 minutes 🕐

Focus

To get students to listen again, this time for specific pieces of information.

Setup

Have students review the questions before listening to the report. Pair neighboring classmates to compare answers. If disagreements arise, replay the report rather than give the answer. In some cases, students may even want to listen a third time.

✪✪ **REACTING TO THE LISTENING**
Suggested Time: 25 minutes 🕐

Focus

To encourage students to analyze the structure of the report; to engage students in a lively discussion of their own life experiences and approaches to discipline.

Setup

For Exercise 1, have students look at the rubric before listening to each excerpt. As they listen, have them write down the speaker's key words. Allow them a few minutes to compose their own summary statements before sharing them with a partner or with the class. Lead the class in a discussion of the question in Exercise 2. Have students from diverse backgrounds form small groups to discuss the questions in Exercise 3.

Expansion/Homework

For a homework assignment, students could write a paragraph response or compose a spoken response in their audio journals to one of the questions in Exercise 3.

✪✪✪ B **LISTENING TWO:** *Describing Monastic Life*

Suggested Time: 25 minutes 🕐

Focus

To present an interview with a journalist who has visited many monasteries around the world.

Setup

Have students read the introductory paragraph and information before listening to the interview. Play the interview once, while students listen with their eyes closed to focus their concentration. Have students listen a second time while they complete the exercise. Review answers as a class. If disagreements arise, replay the interview.

Expansion/Homework

You may want to discuss the following questions as a class: *This interview focuses on monasteries that have had many encounters with the mainstream world. Do you think these monasteries have too much contact with the mainstream world? Why? Why not? What is the purpose of a monastery?*

Link to *NorthStar: Reading and Writing*
Ask students to develop a definition of a monastery based on the shared general characteristics of those described in this unit.

❊❊❊ C LINKING LISTENINGS ONE AND TWO

Suggested Time: 25 minutes ⏺

Focus
To relate the material in the listenings to students' own interests; to connect students' life experiences to the theme of the listenings.

Setup
For Exercise 1, have students read the list of practices and rank them according to each person's preference. Then form groups of three or four students for a continued discussion of their choices. For Exercise 2, have students find new partners to brainstorm reasons why people seek spiritual renewal. Lead a follow-up discussion. Write students' ideas on the board and then ask, *How do these ideas connect to what you learned in this book about Internet addiction, Celebration, Florida, and the Western adaptation of feng shui?*

Expansion/Homework
(1) To promote active use of new words during this activity, you may want to list the vocabulary from Section 1C (Vocabulary for Comprehension) on the board. Or you could create a list by integrating the vocabulary from the Listening/Speaking and Reading/Writing strands. See the Word List for each unit at the end of the Teacher's Manual and on the Companion Website at **http://www.longman.com/northstar**. (2) Students could brainstorm reasons for each of these practices. Refer to Section 2, Listening for Main Ideas, to remind students of the multiple reasons why one might fast. Have pairs of students from different religious backgrounds generate several reasons for the other practices on this page and then share their ideas with the class.

Link to *NorthStar: Reading and Writing*
Ask students to compare the notions on spiritual renewal in this unit and the definition of religion in the companion Unit 6. Ask, *Do these spiritual practices constitute a religion according the definition you read? Is there a difference between religious practice and spiritual practice?*

❸ Focus on Vocabulary, PAGE 130

✪ EXERCISE 1
Suggested Time: 25 minutes ⏺

Focus
To expand students' vocabulary as they learn about the life of Thomas Merton, a celebrated twentieth-century Catholic monk.

Setup

Review the pronunciation of the underlined words. Then have students form pairs (with students from different language backgrounds, if possible) to read the text aloud and match the underlined words and definitions. Check comprehension by asking, *Where was Thomas Merton born? What was his nationality? About how old was he when he converted to Catholicism? Why were close friends and family baffled by his decision to become a monk? What was his great gift? How did he share his gift? What issues concerned him most?*

Expansion/Homework

(1) You could convert the reading portion of these activities into a listening exercise by reading the article to the class and then checking comprehension with the questions listed in Setup. (2) Or, if class time is limited, you may want to assign this exercise as homework and use class time to check answers and work on pronunciation. (3) To help students memorize this vocabulary, have them work in pairs to quiz each other on the definitions. One can play the teacher; the other can play the student. Then have them switch roles.

Link to *NorthStar: Reading and Writing*

Ask students to imagine what the Dali Lama and Thomas Merton discussed in their historical encounter in 1968. Ask, *What did these two men have in common?*

✪ EXERCISE 2
Suggested Time: 15 minutes

Focus

To practice unit vocabulary in a guided conversation about the life and writings of Thomas Merton.

Setup

Have students of similar fluency levels form pairs. Give students a few minutes of preparation time to take notes before they ask and answer the questions about Thomas Merton using the vocabulary listed. To promote the conversational tone of this exercise, remind students to make lots of eye contact with each other.

Expansion/Homework

For homework, students could write a paragraph response or compose a spoken response in their audio journals to question 4.

 For extra vocabulary practice, have students work on the self-grading vocabulary activities for the unit on the NorthStar Companion Website at **http://www.longman.com/northstar**.

4 Focus on Speaking, PAGE 133

✪✪ A PRONUNCIATION: Vowel Alternation

Suggested Time: 20 minutes 🕐

Focus
To practice identifying and pronouncing the long and short vowel sounds of *a, e,* and *i.*

Setup
Read the introductory passage aloud or have students read it silently. For Exercise 1, have the class repeat after you or the audio. Encourage students to look at the way your mouth forms each sound and to mimic your movements. You will need to give students ample practice identifying the vowel sounds. Write the three patterns on the board; say the sets of words in Exercise 1, but in scrambled order. With their books closed, have students listen and identify the vowel patterns. For Exercise 2, have students work in pairs (with students from different language backgrounds, if possible) to pronounce the words and identify their vowel sound patterns. If students aren't familiar with the pronunciation of these words, you will need to read each set aloud as they listen and identify the vowel sound pattern.

Expansion/Homework
In Exercise 1, students could brainstorm longer lists of words that illustrate the vowel shifts. If students need inspiration, prompt them with these suggestions: *sleep, bite, deal, read, rise.*

✪✪ B GRAMMAR: Count and Non-Count Nouns and Their Quantifiers

Suggested Time: 25 minutes 🕐

Focus
To become aware of and practice using tricky count and non-count nouns and their quantifiers; to review concepts presented in this unit; to introduce students to a celebrated Buddhist monk, Tenzin Palmo.

Setup
Have students of different fluency levels work in pairs to examine the sentences and respond to the two prompts that follow. Ask students to read the grammar explanations silently. You may need to give additional examples of the contrast in meaning between *few—a few* and *little—a little.* Continuing with the same partner, have students do Exercise 2. Go over the answers with the class. Students can work on Exercise 3 independently. As students finish, have them compare answers with a partner. Respond to any questions. For Exercise 4, have students find new partners to complete the interview. Ask students to read the whole interview once before filling in the blanks. Check comprehension and ask, *Where is Tenzin Palmo from? Why did she go to India? Did she spend a long time looking for her spiritual master? Why did she live as a hermit? What kind of work does she do now?* When students role play the interview, encourage them to make eye contact.

Expansion/Homework

(1) This whole section works well for homework. Students can go over the answers in class to work on pronunciation. (2) Using the pronunciation skills they learned in Unit 3, students could silently read the completed interview and mark the thought groups before they read their roles aloud. (3) You may want students to further review this material by choosing one topic discussed in this unit (fasting, life in monasteries, spiritual practices, Thomas Merton, Tenzin Palmo) for a short one-minute extemporaneous speech. The listening students can write all the count and non-count nouns they hear. Review their lists as a class. (4) For further practice, offer exercises from *Focus on Grammar, Advanced* and from Azar's *Understanding and Using English Grammar*. See the Grammar Book References on page 247 of the Student Book.

✪✪✪ C STYLE: Telling an Anecdote

Suggested Time: 25 minutes

Focus

To analyze how speakers tell anecdotes; to present an additional portion of the interview with William Claassen (from Listening Two) about life in a forest monastery; to give students the opportunity to practice telling their own anecdotes.

Setup

Ask students to read the introductory paragraph and the questions in Exercise 1 before listening to the excerpt. Explain the meaning of the idiomatic use of *would* (repetitive action in the past). As a class review the expressions in Exercise 2. Brainstorm any other possible phrases or expressions. For Exercise 3, have students individually prepare their anecdotes. In pairs of their own choosing, have students share their stories. Ask students to retell the stories they heard to another classmate or to the whole class.

Expansion/Homework

(1) If possible, have students record the anecdotes in Exercise 3 and then listen to their own performances. They can listen for pronunciation and usage errors, which they can write down and then correct. (2) If taping is not possible, circulate around the room and listen as students speak. Note any errors by using a divided page: Usage/Pronunciation. Have students correct the usage errors and mark the pronunciation words with stress marks over the stressed syllables. Circulate around the room, answering students' questions. As a class, you can review the pronunciation of some of the most frequent errors.

 For extra listening practice, have students use the NorthStar Companion Video.

✪✪✪ D SPEAKING TOPIC

Focus

To integrate the concepts, vocabulary, pronunciation skills (vowel alternation), grammar (count and non-count nouns and their quantifiers), and style focus (telling anecdotes) of the unit in a role play debate; to explore a case study, based on fact, which probes the complex question of how monasteries should relate to the "mainstream" world.

Setup

Ask students to read the case study in small groups or independently. Check comprehension and ask, *What is the monks' schedule? What shape was Mepkin in when the abbot arrived? How did the abbot revitalize Mepkin? What is the new proposal? Who supports the new proposal? Why? Who is against the new proposal? Why?* Have the class divide into two groups. Have members of each group take on roles specific to the case (monks, abbot, neighbors, visitors, the elderly, business owners, farmers). Have students develop their arguments and identify the pros and cons. Then have the class conduct a debate. You could be moderator to ensure that each side gets equal time in presenting and rebutting arguments.

Expansion/Homework:

(1) You could convert the reading portion of these activities into a listening exercise by reading the article to the class and then checking comprehension with the questions listed in Setup. (2) During the debate, take note of the most salient usage and pronunciation errors, and comment on the content and delivery of ideas. You can then distribute these notes to the individual students. Have them return the papers to you with the usage errors corrected and the pronunciation words marked with stress marks over the stressed syllables. As a class, review the pronunciation of the most frequent errors. (3) For homework, students could write an opinion on the Mepkin case from the point of view of one of the characters and record it in their audio journals.

✪ E RESEARCH TOPICS

Focus

To research one of the themes presented in this unit.

Setup

Review the topics with the class. In pairs of their own choosing, have students research one topic and present their findings to the class.

Expansion/Homework

(1) If you live in an English-speaking community and you or the students know a person who is a member of a monastery or religious community, invite the person to speak to the class. Each student can write at least one question to pose to the guest. You may want to review the questions as a class to eliminate redundancy. (2) For further reading on this topic, the following texts are

recommended: *Alone in Community: Journeys into Monastic Life around the World*, by William Claassen; *New Seeds of Contemplation*, by Thomas Merton; and *In the Spirit of Happiness*, by The Monks of New Skete (editor).

Link to *NorthStar: Reading and Writing*

If time allows, you could do a speaking topic from Section 4D (in class) and a writing topic (at home). You will probably want to choose the research topic that fits your students and the classroom environment best. When students speak, remind them to use vocabulary and examples from the Reading/Writing material on world faiths.

Workplace Privacy

OVERVIEW	
Theme:	Business

Listenings:	Listening One: *Interview on Workplace Surveillance*
	    Interviews with workplace specialists
	Listening Two: *Managers and Employees Speak Out about*
	    Workplace Privacy
	    Two opposing points of view

Critical Thinking Skills:	Infer meaning not explicit in text Compare and contrast cultural norms of privacy Establish personal standards of privacy Support opinions with information from the text Hypothesize another's point of view Speculate on outcomes of a case Analyze two cases Compare and contrast word usage and meaning Extract logical arguments from the text to defend a position
Listening Tasks:	Listen for main ideas Listen for details Interpret speaker's intensity of feeling Take detailed notes using a graphic organizer Relate listening to personal values Integrate information from both listenings Listen for correct stress in verbs and nouns Listen for logical arguments in a listening text
Speaking Tasks:	Brainstorm words about privacy Make predictions Construct and perform a dialogue Practice correct stress patterns in extemporaneous responses Act out a scripted interview Respond extemporaneously to prompts using words and phrases to frame an argument Debate with classmates Interview people and summarize findings
Pronunciation:	Stress on two-syllable words
Vocabulary:	Context clues Definitions Synonyms
Grammar:	Verb + gerund or infinitive—two forms, two meanings

UNIT SUMMARY

This unit explores the issue of workplace privacy and the growing surveillance of employees. Listening One is a news report on the alarming rise of secret monitoring of employees on the job. Listening Two explores different perspectives of employers and employees on the issue of workplace surveillance.

The companion unit in *NorthStar: Reading and Writing* explores the advantages and disadvantage of starting a career by working for a large firm or starting up a business on one's own.

1 Focus on the Topic, PAGE 145

✪✪✪ A PREDICTING

Suggested Time: 10 minutes

Focus
To get students thinking about the issue of workplace privacy and some of the related ideas and vocabulary.

Setup
Ask students to read the title and the cartoon and discuss the questions with a neighboring classmate. Then allow students two minutes to write their associations with the word *privacy*. Elicit their ideas and write them on the board.

Expansion/Homework
You may want to ask students, *How many monitoring devices can you find in this picture? What is the purpose of each device? What kind of employer might install these kinds of devices?*

✪✪ B SHARING INFORMATION

Suggested Time: 20 minutes

Focus
To get students to discuss freely their opinions and experiences related to privacy; to elicit cultural differences in experience.

Setup
Have students from varied cultural backgrounds form small groups to discuss the questions. Have students share with the class any interesting insights they heard in their group discussions.

✪✪✪ C **PREPARING TO LISTEN**

BACKGROUND
Suggested Time: 20 minutes 🕐

Focus
To introduce students to the issue of workplace privacy; to awaken interest in and aid comprehension of the listening that follows.

Setup
Have students read the text individually. Check comprehension by asking, *What is the employee's perspective on the issue of workplace privacy? What is the employer's position? What laws exist in the United States now to protect citizens' privacy? What is the key issue in employees' right to privacy?* Have students respond individually to the statements and then pair up (with a student from a different employment background, if possible) to discuss their opinions.

Expansion/Homework
(1) You may want to assign this section as homework. Then students can discuss their opinions as a class. (2) You could convert the reading into a listening exercise by reading the text aloud as students listen. Check their comprehension with the questions listed in Setup. (3) This reading can be used as a jigsaw: Photocopy the text and then cut out the paragraphs. Give students a paragraph to read and have them take notes. With only notes in hand, have students in groups of four explain their paragraphs to each other. To check comprehension, have students respond to the questions listed in Setup. (4) To add challenge to the discussion, insist that the students come to a consensus on the statements on workplace privacy. (5) Encourage your students to follow this topic in the news or online. Have them bring articles they find that mention workplace privacy to class.

VOCABULARY FOR COMPREHENSION
Suggested Time: 15 minutes 🕐

Focus
To acquaint students with issues in workplace privacy as well as the vocabulary necessary to talk about these issues; to aid listening comprehension.

Setup
As a class, practice pronouncing the highlighted words. Have students work in groups (with four to five students from different language backgrounds, if possible) to read the talk show script aloud (1 host, 4 callers). Encourage them to read the script dramatically, using intonation, stress, and gestures to dramatize their performance. Then have students find the matching expressions. Go over the answers as a class, with students reading them aloud so you can correct pronunciation.

Expansion/Homework
(1) Using the pronunciation skills they learned in Unit 3, students could silently read the completed talk show and mark the thought groups before they read their roles aloud. (2) If class time is limited, you may want to assign this section as homework and use class time to check answers and work on pronunciation.

✪✪✪ 2 Focus on Listening, PAGE 150

✪✪✪ **A** █ **LISTENING ONE:** *Interview on Workplace Surveillance*
Suggested Time: 10 minutes ⏱

Focus
To get students to predict the reasons workplace surveillance is on the rise; to help students predict the contents of the news report.

Setup
Have students work with a partner to list reasons for the rise of workplace surveillance. To encourage use of the vocabulary learned in Section 1C, write the words on the board for students' reference. Have students listen to the excerpt and compare that list with their own. Ask students to share any reactions with the class.

Expansion/Homework
As a class, you may want to elicit ideas and write them on the board for students' reference after listening to the excerpt.

✪✪✪ LISTENING FOR MAIN IDEAS
Suggested Time: 20 minutes ⏱

Focus
To help students listen for the main ideas in an extended report on workplace privacy.

Setup
Have students read the questions before listening. Clarify any vocabulary. Play Parts One, Two, and Three, pausing after each part so students can complete their writing. Have students compare answers with a neighboring classmate. If disagreements arise, play each part again.

Expansion/Homework
To challenge more advanced students, convert Listening One into a note-taking activity. With books closed, have students take notes using a divided page: Main Ideas/Details. Then have students pair up with a neighboring classmate to compare notes. When finished, students can open their books and answer the questions.

✪✪✪ LISTENING FOR DETAILS
Suggested Time: 20 minutes ⏱

Focus
To get students to listen carefully again, this time for specific information.

Setup
First have students read the true/false statements and respond to the ones they already know. Play the news report again, letting students compare answers after each part. If disagreements arise, replay the segment rather than give the answer.

In some cases, students may even want to listen a third time. This is a particularly challenging text.

Expansion/Homework

You could also have groups of three students quiz each other, reading the statements aloud. Each student can read one part aloud to the group. To aid in their exchanges, you may want to write phrases for expressing opinions on the board (*I think . . . /I disagree . . . /Don't you think that . . .*)

✪✪ REACTING TO THE LISTENING
Suggested Time: 25 minutes ⏲

Focus

To encourage students to interpret the tone of a speaker's voice and make inferences about the speaker's strength of conviction; to encourage students to think and consider several possibilities in their responses.

Setup

For Exercise 1, have students read the items before they listen to the excerpts. Allow them a few minutes to think about their responses before discussing them with a partner. If there is disagreement, welcome it. Encourage students to support their points of view with details from the interview. Emphasize that it is possible for students to have varying opinions, as long as their reasoning is sound. After each excerpt, have the pairs share any especially interesting observations they made with the class. For Exercise 2, have students individually read the questions and write their responses before you lead the class discussion.

Expansion/Homework

(1) You may want to bring in a video or audio clip of a news editorial for students to evaluate in terms of strength of opinion expressed. A good source for such material comes from C-SPAN's coverage of legislators' one-minute speeches. (2) You could also have students express their own opinions about workplace privacy in small groups. They can use the opinions listed in Background, Section 1C, as prompts. As students listen to each speaker in their group, have them take note of any words or expressions that indicate the intensity of the speaker's convictions. Then have students give their feedback to the speaker. (3) The questions in Exercise 2 are also relevant to the context of citizens concerned about their right to privacy and a government's need to maintain national security. Have students answer these questions again, this time not as employees, but rather as citizens. Have students compare their tolerance for security measures imposed by an employer with security measures imposed by a government.

✪✪✪ B LISTENING TWO: *Managers and Employees Speak Out*

Suggested Time: 25 minutes

Focus
To give students more perspectives on the issue of workplace privacy; to expose students to informal speech.

Setup
Go over the chart with the class. Play the interview one time with books closed. Suggest that students shut their eyes to focus their concentration. Then have students fill in the chart as they listen a second time. Have students form small groups (with students from different cultural backgrounds, if possible) to discuss their reactions to the opinions presented in the interview.

Link to *NorthStar: Reading and Writing*
Ask, *How do you think the young entrepreneurs Larry Page, Tina Wells, Dineh Monajer, and Matt Kelly would feel about workplace privacy?* Ask students to write a paragraph statement from the perspective of one of these entrepreneurs.

✪✪✪ C LINKING LISTENINGS ONE AND TWO

Suggested Time: 25 minutes

Focus
To get students to apply their understandings of the two listenings to two workplace privacy scenarios; to encourage students to identify the advantages and disadvantages of a situation; to add information about other ways in which privacy is compromised at work.

Setup
Have students of varying ages and experiences work in small groups to read the scenarios and respond to the questions that follow. Remind students to refrain from expressing their own opinions until they fully understand each party's perspective on the issue. Encourage use of vocabulary learned in this unit by writing the words on the board for students' reference. Have students share their ideas with the class.

Expansion/Homework
(1) Before beginning this section, you may want students to restate orally each listening in pairs, small groups, or as a class, to help strengthen their overall grasp of the material. (2) Listen as students discuss the scenarios and note any errors on a divided page: Usage/Pronunciation. You can then distribute these notes to the groups of students. Have them return the papers to you with the usage errors corrected and the pronunciation words marked with stress marks over the stressed syllables. As a class, you can review the pronunciation of the most frequent errors.

3 Focus on Vocabulary, PAGE 156

✪ EXERCISE 1
Suggested Time: 30 minutes ⊚

Focus
To give students more practice with the vocabulary in this unit; to introduce a real court case of Nissan employees accusing their boss of monitoring their private communications.

Setup
As a class, practice pronouncing the new vocabulary. Then have students work with a partner (someone from a different language background, if possible) to complete the exercises. Encourage them to consult each other and their dictionaries before consulting you. Check students' comprehension of the passage by asking, *What did Rhonda Hall and Bonita Bourke correspond about in their e-mail? How did their boss spy on them? Why were they fired? Why did the women file a formal complaint against Nissan?*

Expansion/Homework
If class time is limited, you may want to assign this exercise as homework and use class time to check answers and work on pronunciation.

✪ EXERCISES 2 AND 3
Suggested Time: 30 minutes ⊚

Focus
To use the vocabulary in this unit in a dramatization of the court case; to analyze a case and predict its outcome.

Setup
For Exercise 2, give students plenty of time to write the dialogue and practice it before they present it dramatically to the class. Bring props (such as a tie, desk apparatus, and a Nissan sign) to set the stage for the students' performance. For Exercise 3, have small groups of students predict the outcome of the Bourke versus Nissan case and then provide them with the outcome explained on page 243 of the Student Book.

Expansion/Homework
(1) To provide students with feedback, you may want to videotape or audiorecord this role play. Students can then listen to their role play and identify errors to correct. (2) If taping is not possible, take notes on pronunciation and usage as they perform their role plays. After commenting on the strengths of their role play, write the usage errors on the board (or overhead projector) and invite students to correct the errors. For pronunciation correction, write the words to be practiced on the board, invite the class to identify the stressed syllables, model the pronunciation, and encourage students to practice repeating each word or phrase until they are confident of their own pronunciation. (3) You may want to do Exercise 3 as a class, eliciting students' ideas to put on the

board and then reading the resolution from the Answer Key aloud to the class. Ask students for their reactions.

 For extra vocabulary practice, have students work on the self-grading vocabulary activities for the unit on the NorthStar Companion Website at **http://www.longman.com/northstar**.

4 Focus on Speaking, PAGE 159

✪✪A   PRONUNCIATION: Stress on Two-Syllable Words

Suggested Time: 20 minutes

Focus
To expand and reinforce unit vocabulary; to get students to recognize and produce the different stress patterns of verbs and nouns.

Setup
Read the introductory statement aloud or have students read it silently. Have students listen to the audio and identify the stressed syllables of the underlined words. Model the pronunciation of the underlined words. Point out that two-syllable nouns tend to receive the stress on the first syllable, whereas two-syllable verbs tend to receive the stress on the second syllable. Also point out how the stressed vowel tends to be a clear, open, and long vowel, and how the unstressed vowel tends to be reduced, closed, and short. Have students from different language backgrounds work in pairs to complete Exercises 2 and 3. Go over the answers with the class to work on pronunciation.

Expansion/Homework
(1) Some students can grasp stress better if it is acompanied with a gesture; the physical movement focuses attention on the cadence of the word. You can have students swing their hands, shift their weight, or stomp their feet to reflect the stressed syllable of a word. (2) You may want to give students additional practice by having them make their own statements about the theme of workplace privacy using the underlined words. As students listen, they can identify the words as nouns or verbs. (3) You may want to invite students to come up with their own pairs of verbs and nouns to present to the class.

✪✪✪B   GRAMMAR: Verb + Gerund or Infinitive—Two Forms, Two Meanings

Suggested Time: 25 minutes

Focus
To acquaint students with verbs that change meaning when followed by a gerund or an infinitive; to practice using these verbs in speaking as students review the information and vocabulary used in this unit.

Setup

Have students of different fluency levels work in pairs to examine the sentences in Exercise 1 and answer the two questions that follow. Ask students to read the grammar explanations silently. Have students work individually on Exercise 2. As students finish, have them compare answers with a partner. Respond to any questions. For Exercise 3, have students from different language backgrounds complete the script and then read it dramatically as a role play.

Expansion/Homework

(1) If class time is limited, Exercises 1 and 2 can be assigned for homework. In class, students compare answers and work on pronunciation. (2) Using the pronunciation skills they learned in Unit 3, students could silently read Exercise 3 and mark the thought groups before they read their roles aloud. (3) You may want students to further review this material by using at least three of the underlined words in this section to tell each other anecdotes. The students listening can write all the verbs they hear from this section. Review the lists as a class. (4) For further practice, offer exercises from *Focus on Grammar, Advanced* and from Azar's *Understanding and Using English Grammar*. See the Grammar Book References on page 248 of the Student Book.

✪✪✪C STYLE: Framing an Argument

Suggested Time: 25 minutes

Focus

To get students to practice expressions for framing an oral argument; to practice expressing opinions on the information in this unit.

Setup

Have students read the examples silently. Model the phrases with lively intonation and have students repeat until they are confident of their own pronunciation and intonation. Pair stronger and weaker students together to do the exercise. Allow them a few minutes to read the information and prepare notes for reference. Meanwhile, write the phrases on the board for easy reference. Encourage students to make eye contact and use gestures to enhance the expression of opinion in these exchanges. Invite students to add their own points as they frame their arguments.

Expansion/Homework

Have each pair stand up in front of the class and deliver a dramatic exchange modeled on one of the points. Be sure they use stress, intonation, and gestures to strengthen the argument they present. Offer individual written corrections to each student.

For extra listening practice, have students use the NorthStar Companion Video.

✪✪✪ **D**   ▐ **SPEAKING TOPIC**

Focus
To integrate the concepts, vocabulary, pronunciation skills (stress on two-syllable words), grammar (verb + gerund or infinitive), and style focus (framing an argument) of the unit; to conduct a debate on an employee monitoring law.

Setup
Have students listen to the audio and then read the interview. Divide the class into two teams: for and against the employee monitoring law. Give the teams a few minutes to develop their arguments. Meanwhile, write the phrases for framing an argument from page 164, as well as the verbs from page 161, on the board for reference. During the debate, you can play the role of impartial timekeeper and protocol enforcer. Have the teams take timed turns offering opening statements, position points, rebuttals, and conclusions. Conduct a debriefing session after the debate to hear students' reactions to the case.

Expansion/Homework
(1) You may want to have two student volunteers read the interview dramatically to the class as everyone listens with books closed. (2) You may want to videorecord the debate. Use it to have students appreciate and react to their work. You may want to ask for a written reaction paragraph: How did you feel watching yourself speak English? What did you do well? What skills need work? (3) During the debate, take notes of the most salient usage and pronunciation errors. When the debate is finished, present your notes—either for the class or for each individual student—and invite students to correct the errors. For pronunciation correction, write the words to be practiced on the board, invite the class to identify the stressed syllables, model the pronunciation, and encourage students to practice repeating each word or phrase until they are confident of their own pronunciation.

✪ **E**   ▐ **RESEARCH TOPIC**

Focus
To elicit opinions on workplace privacy in roving-reporter-style interviews; to find out how local people feel about this issue.

Setup
You may want to work on interview techniques with the students. Review the expressions in the Style section (4C) of Unit 3, "Starting a Conversation and Keeping It Going," on page 66. Help the students brainstorm different ways to signal interest and concern during the interview. In pairs of their own choosing, have students identify two workplaces in which to conduct interviews and develop questions to ask. Discuss the possibility that some people may be unwilling to be interviewed and why. Have them do the interview together and then report their findings to the class.

Expansion/Homework

(**1**) If you live in an English-speaking context, you might want to invite an employee and an employer from the same workplace to speak to the class about monitoring employees. Each student can write at least two questions to pose to the guests. You may want to review the questions as a class to eliminate redundancy. (**2**) For further reading on this topic, the following texts are recommended: *The Right to Privacy*, by Ellen Alderman and Caroline Kennedy; and *Private Matters: In Defense of the Personal Life*, by Janna Malamud Smith.

Link to *NorthStar: Reading and Writing*

If time allows, you could do a speaking topic from Section 4D (in class) and a writing topic (at home). You will probably want to assign the research topic that fits your students and the classroom environment best. When students speak, remind them to use vocabulary from the Reading/Writing material on starting a career on one's own.

Warriors without Weapons

OVERVIEW

Theme:	The Military

Listenings:	Listening One: *Warriors without Weapons*
	    An interview with a scholar of the Geneva Conventions
	Listening Two: *Michael's Ignatieff's Views on War*
	    More excerpts from the interview

Critical Thinking Skills:	Infer information not explicit in the text Evaluate own understanding of the text Infer word meaning from context Draw conclusions based on information in the interview Illustrate abstract concepts with concrete examples Support opinions with information from the interview Make judgments on controversial issues Hypothesize qualities of an ICRC recruit
Listening Tasks:	Take notes on main ideas Listen for details Listen closely to interpret meaning from word usage Interpret speaker's tone and attitude Relate listening to personal values and opinions Listen for specific information in classmate responses Complete an aural cloze Categorize vowel sounds Listen to a public service announcement and take notes
Speaking Tasks:	Make predictions Compare background experiences React to a text using functional language Express and defend opinions Pose and respond to questions using new vocabulary Retell a conversation Respond extemporaneously to complex questions using words and phrases to stall and elucidate Develop and perform a public service announcement
Pronunciation:	Vowels /æ/, /a/, /ə/ Tongue twisters
Vocabulary:	Context clues Synonyms Definitions Confusing pairs
Grammar:	Direct and indirect speech

UNIT SUMMARY

This unit deals with the International Committee of the Red Cross (ICRC): its history, mission, services, and controversial position of wartime neutrality. Listening One is a wide-ranging and thought-provoking interview with an author of several publications on the ICRC. Listening Two explores the author's perspective on the morality and nature of war.

The companion unit in *NorthStar: Reading and Writing* explores the experiences of women in the military.

1 Focus on the Topic, PAGE 169

✪✪✪A PREDICTING

Suggested Time: 10 minutes ⏰

Focus
To familiarize students with the Geneva Conventions and the International Committee of the Red Cross.

Setup
Ask students to read the title, the cartoon, and the question before forming small groups to discuss their responses. Have the groups share their ideas with the class.

Expansion/Homework
You may want to elicit responses from the class and write them on the board. Students may want to refer to these notes in the subsequent exercises (Sections 1C and 2A) to check the accuracy of their initial predictions.

✪✪B SHARING INFORMATION

Suggested Time: 20 minutes ⏰

Focus
To get students to discuss freely their experiences in volunteering, emergency care, and war.

Setup
Have students read the items before working with a partner to answer the questions. Then, to enrich this discussion, have students of varying ages and experiences form groups. Have students share any interesting experiences they heard described in their group discussions.

Expansion/Homework
(1) You may want to have students who checked one of the items deliver a short one-minute talk to the class describing their experiences. (2) You could also have

students interview someone outside of the classroom who has experienced one of the items and report their findings to the class.

✪✪✪ C   PREPARING TO LISTEN

BACKGROUND
Suggested Time: 20 minutes 🕐

Focus
To introduce students to the mission and activities of the ICRC and other humanitarian relief organizations; to reflect on what students have learned; to awaken interest in and aid comprehension of the listening that follows.

Setup
Have students read the text in Exercise 1 individually. Check comprehension by asking, *Is the ICRC a Swiss agency? What are some of the ICRC's peacetime activities? Why are the ICRC's wartime activities controversial? In what circumstances do other humanitarian agencies not maintain neutrality?* Have students write responses to the questions and then check their answers by rereading the text. Have students take the quiz, and then provide them with the answers from the Answer Key. Ask for their reactions. For Exercise 2, have students form pairs to discuss their reactions.

Expansion/Homework
(1) If class time is limited, you may want to assign Exercise 1 as homework. Then students can discuss their reactions in class. (2) You could convert the reading into a listening exercise by reading the text aloud as students listen. Check their comprehension with the questions listed in Setup. (3) Encourage your students to follow this topic in the news or online. Have them bring any articles they find that mention the ICRC to class.

VOCABULARY FOR COMPREHENSION
Suggested Time: 15 minutes 🕐

Focus
To introduce vocabulary and aid listening comprehension; to acquaint students with a brief history of the ICRC.

Setup
As a class, practice pronouncing the underlined words. Have students read the passage individually. Check comprehension by asking, *Who was Jean-Henri Dunant? What inspired him to set up the Geneva Conventions? What did his critics say? About how many nations subscribe to the Geneva Conventions?* Then have students work in pairs (with students from different language backgrounds, if possible) to find the matching expressions. Go over the answers as a class, with students reading them aloud so you can correct pronunciation.

Expansion/Homework

(1) You may want to assign this section as homework and then use class time to check answers and work on pronunciation. (2) To help students memorize vocabulary, have them work in pairs to quiz each other on the definitions. One can play the teacher; the other can play the student. Then have them switch roles. (3) You could convert the reading into a listening exercise by reading the text aloud as students listen. Check their comprehension with the questions listed in Setup.

2 Focus on Listening, PAGE 173

✪✪✪ A LISTENING ONE: *Warriors without Weapons*

Suggested Time: 10 minutes ⏱

Focus
To get students to predict the contents of an interview with a journalist who has researched the work of Red Cross relief workers and the laws of war.

Setup
Have students work with a partner to list topics they expect to hear about in this interview. To encourage use of the vocabulary learned in Section 1C, write the words on the board for students' reference. Have students listen to the excerpt and compare that list with their own. Ask students to share any reactions with the class.

Expansion/Homework
As a class, you may want to elicit ideas and write them on the board for reference after listening to the excerpt.

✪✪✪ LISTENING FOR MAIN IDEAS

Suggested Time: 20 minutes ⏱

Focus
To help students listen for the main ideas in an extended interview with an expert on the ICRC.

Setup
Have students read the key phrases before they listen to the interview. Play Parts One, Two, and Three, pausing after each part so students can complete their writing. Have students compare answers with a neighboring classmate. If disagreements arise, play each part again.

Expansion/Homework
You could ask students to use the key phrases and their notes to make an oral summary of the listening.

✪✪✪ LISTENING FOR DETAILS
Suggested Time: 20 minutes 🕐

Focus
To get students to listen carefully again, this time for specific pieces of information.

Setup
First have students read the multiple-choice questions, responding to the ones they can already answer. Play the interview, letting students compare answers after each part. If disagreements arise, replay the segment rather than give the answer. In some cases, students may want to listen several times.

✪✪ REACTING TO THE LISTENING
Suggested Time: 25 minutes 🕐

Focus
To encourage students to interpret information and make inferences about the interview; to encourage students to think and consider several possibilities in their responses; to promote critical discussion of and reflection on the interview.

Setup
Have students read the questions in Exercise 1 before they listen to the excerpts. Allow students a few minutes to think about their responses before discussing them with a partner (someone from a different language background, if possible). If there is disagreement, welcome it. Encourage students to support their points of view with details from the interview. Emphasize that it is possible for students to have varying opinions, as long as their reasoning is sound. Have pairs report to the class any interesting observations they made. To prepare for Exercise 2, call on individual students to restate the issues presented in the interview. Then have students individually read and react to the statements. In small groups of students of varying ages, have students discuss their opinions.

Expansion/Homework
For Exercise 2, you may want to aid students' discussion by writing on the board phrases from the section on Framing Arguments in Unit 7 (page 164).

✪✪✪ B ▐ LISTENING TWO: *Michael Ignatieff's Views on War*
Suggested Time: 20 minutes 🕐

Focus
To give students a moral interpretation of war by listening to Michael Ignatieff describe his evolving understanding of war: its function, limits, and conventions; to explore the question of how experience can lead to a change of heart.

Setup
Go over the items with the class. Have students check them off as they listen to the excerpts. You may need to replay the interview several times.

Expansion/Homework
You may want students to read the items and predict how Michael Ignatieff will respond before they listen to the interview.

✪✪✪ C **LINKING LISTENINGS ONE AND TWO**

Suggested Time: 25 minutes

Focus
To get students to remember and interpret information from the two listenings; to get students to apply their understanding of the second listening by creating a dialogue between Michael Ignatieff and a pacifist friend.

Setup
Have students of varying ages form groups to discuss the questions. To encourage use of the vocabulary learned earlier in the unit, write the words from Section 1C on the board for students' reference. You may want to ask the groups to share any interesting opinions or insights from their discussions.

Expansion/Homework
(1) As students discuss their opinions, listen and write any errors on a divided page: Usage/Pronunciation. Have students return the papers to you with the usage errors corrected and the pronunciation words marked with stress marks over the stressed syllables. As a class, you can review the pronunciation of the most frequent errors. (2) For homework, students could write a paragraph response or compose an audio journal response to one of the questions. (3) Students could debate question 3 as a class.

Link to _NorthStar: Reading and Writing_
The Gulf War soldiers sent letters home describing the "death and destruction" of war. Ask students, _What rules of war did they fear would be broken? One soldier gave an example of warrior honor. What was it?_

3 Focus on Vocabulary, PAGE 179

✪ **EXERCISES 1 AND 2**
Suggested Time: 25 minutes

Focus
To expand and reinforce unit vocabulary; to get students to distinguish between words that are similar in sound and spelling, yet distinct in meaning and function.

Setup
Have students read the examples and the explanation. Model the pronunciation of the confusing pairs. Have students work individually to complete Exercise 2 and then check their answers with a classmate or in a small group.

Expansion/Homework

(1) Exercise 2 can be converted into a listening/speaking exercise by having pairs of students take turns reading the sentences aloud. The student who listens covers the sentences and then identifies the correct definition. (2) Or, if class time is limited, you may want to assign Exercise 2 for homework. (3) You could invite students to come up with other confusing pairs to present to the class.

✪ EXERCISE 3
Suggested Time: 25 minutes

Focus

To practice new vocabulary in a guided conversation about the ICRC and the laws of war.

Setup

Have students work in pairs (with students from different language backgrounds, if possible) to ask and answer the questions. Model the first one so that students understand that Student A has the correct information and that Student B must cover the information and only listen to the prompt. When students finish the first part, have them switch roles.

✪ EXERCISES 4 AND 5
Suggested Time: 30 minutes

Focus

To give students more practice with the vocabulary in this unit; to add depth to the topic with two editorial letters defending and opposing the ICRC practice of wartime neutrality.

Setup

As a class, practice pronouncing the underlined vocabulary in Exercise 4. Then have students work individually to complete the exercise. Go over answers aloud to check pronunciation. For Exercise 5, have students work with a partner (someone from a different language background, if possible) to complete the letter. Model the first line so that students understand that Student A needs to read several words beyond the blank space for Student B to be able to identify the missing word. When they finish the first part, have the partners switch jobs.

Expansion/Homework

(1) You may want to assign Exercises 4 as homework and use class time to check answers and work on pronunciation. (2) Students could write editorial letters to the *Star Daily* expressing their opinion on the ICRC's practice of wartime neutrality. (3) To give further vocabulary practice, have small groups of students compete to use twelve words from Section 1C and these exercises to review the ideas in this unit. The first team to finish wins the game. Have one student be note taker. When everyone has finished, ask for sample sentences to check usage.

For extra vocabulary practice, have students work on the self-grading vocabulary activities for the unit on the NorthStar Companion Website at **http://www.longman.com/northstar**.

4 Focus on Speaking, PAGE 185

✪✪ A | PRONUNCIATION: Vowels /æ/, /ɑ/, /ə/

Suggested Time: 25 minutes 🔊

Focus
To identify and practice the short vowel sounds /æ/, /ɑ/, /ə/.

Setup
For Exercise 1, play the audio or have students watch you as you model the words. For Exercise 2, play the audio or say the words yourself. Encourage students to look at how your mouth forms each sound. Identify the origin of each sound; /ɑ/ is formed in the middle of the mouth; and /ə/ originates in the lower back part of the mouth. For Exercise 3, play the audio again as students circle the words they hear. Non-native speakers often struggle to discriminate between the /ɑ/ in *cot* and the /ə/ in *cut*. Students may need additional practice as you say words and they circle the vowel sound they hear. For Exercise 4, have pairs of students from different language backgrounds listen to each other pronounce the words. Model Exercise 5; write the five patterns on the board and choose several phrases for students to classify. Point out that in English the sound-symbol correspondence is not stable. For example, in the word *government* the o sounds like a *u* /ə/. Then have students return to their partners to pronounce the words and identify their vowel sound patterns. If students aren't familiar with the pronunciation of these words, you will need to read them aloud as they listen and identify the vowel sound pattern. For Exercise 6, play the tongue twisters or model them for the class. Encourage students to have fun as they tackle these "vowel" twisters.

Expansion/Homework
(1) You may want students to review one of the paragraphs in the Background text in Section 1C to identify all the vowels that sound like /æ/, then /ɑ/, and then /ə/. (2) Encourage students to use their developing knowledge of the IPA to look up several words in the dictionary.

✪✪ B | GRAMMAR: Direct and Indirect Speech

Suggested Time: 25 minutes 🔊

Focus
To have students practice the transformation from direct to indirect speech; to add depth to the unit theme with dialogues between POWs and ICRC volunteers.

Setup
Have the class examine the paragraph in Exercise 1 and answer the two questions that follow. Ask students to read the grammar explanations silently. Pair students of similar fluency levels to do Exercise 2. Model the first sentence,

The Red Cross volunteer said hello and asked the POW how he was doing. He explained he was there to collect messages for the prisoner's family. Circulate around the room to answer questions as students work on the dialogues.

Expansion/Homework

(1) If class time is limited, you could assign Exercise 1 for homework. (2) You may want to provide additional practice by reading or playing lines from the transcript, which students can then transform into reported speech. (3) For further practice, offer exercises from *Focus on Grammar, Advanced* and from Azar's *Understanding and Using English Grammar.* See the Grammar Book References on page 248 of the Student Book.

✪✪✪ C STYLE: Responding to Complex or Controversial Questions

Suggested Time: 25 minutes

Focus

To get students to practice responding to complex or controversial questions while discussing the information in this unit; to model and promote the practice of "buying time" when one is speaking.

Setup

Have students read the introductory passage and examples silently. Model the phrases with lively intonation and have students repeat them until they are confident of their own pronunciation and intonation. Pair stronger and weaker students together to do the exercise. Allow them a few minutes to read the information and prepare reference notes. Meanwhile, write the phrases on the board for easy reference. Encourage use of eye contact and gestures to enhance the interaction in these exchanges.

Expansion/Homework

(1) If possible, have students record these exchanges and then listen to their own performances. Identify pronunciation and usage errors, which they can write down and then correct. (2) If recording is not possible, circulate around the room and listen to the students' dialogues. Note any errors on a divided page: Usage/Pronunciation. Have students correct the usage errors and mark the pronunciation words with stress marks over the stressed syllables. Answer any student questions. As a class, review the pronunciation of the most frequent errors. (3) Review this exercise as a class. Ask individual students one of the tough questions. Encourage the student to buy time to compose a thoughtful answer.

 For extra listening practice, have students use the NorthStar Companion Video.

✪✪✪ D | SPEAKING TOPIC

Focus

To integrate the concepts, vocabulary, pronunciation skills (vowels /æ/, /ɑ/, and /ə/), grammar (direct and indirect speech), and style focus (responding to complex or controversial questions) of the unit to write and produce a PSA encouraging blood donation.

Setup

To open the activity, ask students, *Have you ever donated blood? For yourself? For others?* Briefly discuss their responses as a class. Be sensitive to strong personal and/or cultural reactions to the topic. Have students read the questions before they listen. Have them listen again and complete the outline. In small groups of their own choosing, have them design and produce their own PSAs using the outline as a guide. Have them videotape or audiorecord their PSAs and then present them to the class. Remind students to do several practice runs before they record the PSA. If no recording equipment is available, have students perform their PSAs instead.

Expansion/Homework

(1) When presenting the PSAs, have the class listen for the information outlined in this section. Encourage them to appreciate their classmates' work, giving constructive feedback on content. (2) During each performance, take note of the strengths of the performers and the most salient usage and pronunciation errors. You can then distribute these notes to the groups. Have them return the papers to you with the usage errors corrected and the pronunciation words marked with stress marks over the stressed syllables. As a class, you can review the pronunciation of some of the most frequent errors. (3) Students may be interested in finding out how to give blood in their communities. Have them call their hospitals or the Red Cross and report their findings to the class.

✪ E | RESEARCH TOPICS

Focus

To practice research and reporting skills as students learn about their local Red Cross office; to research human rights groups on the Internet and to compare the findings with what students have learned about the ICRC.

Setup

For the first aid research, have students work in pairs or small groups of their own choosing. Make sure each group chooses a different theme. Have students conduct their research on the Internet or at a local Red Cross office. Have each group teach the class how to perform that first aid procedure. Encourage a relaxed and fun exchange. For the Internet research, have students form groups of their own choosing. Again, make sure each group chooses a different agency. Before students set out to compare these agencies to the ICRC, you may want to brainstorm with the class the key components of the ICRC. This way all students will share a "core knowledge" of the ICRC with which they can compare their findings.

Expansion/Homework

(1) If you live in an English-speaking community, you might want to invite a Red Cross volunteer or representative to speak to the class about the local Red Cross office and its services. Each student can write at least one question to pose to the guest. You may want to review their questions as a class to eliminate redundancy. (2) For further reading on this topic, the following texts are recommended: *Blood Rites: Origins and History of the Passions of War*, by Barbara Ehrenreich; *The International Committee of the Red Cross*, by David P. Forsythe; and *The Warrior's Honor*, by Michael Ignatieff.

Link to *NorthStar: Reading and Writing*

If time allows, you could do a speaking topic from Section 4D (in class) and a writing topic (at home). You will probably want to choose the research topic that fits your students and the classroom environment best. When students write, remind them to use vocabulary and examples from the Reading/Writing material on women in the military.

Boosting Brain Power through the Arts

OVERVIEW

Theme:	The Arts

Listenings:	Listening One: *Does Music Enhance Math Skills?*
	    A news report
	Listening Two: *Music, Art, and the Brain*
	    An interview with a science journalist

Critical Thinking Skills:	Compare and contrast information Infer word meaning from context Evaluate proposals using criteria set forth in the report Hypothesize alternative ways to boost intelligence Judge the value and benefits of teaching the arts Analyze the pros and cons of education proposals Frame arguments for and against an issue Write a persuasive letter arguing a point of view
Listening Tasks:	Listen to student summaries and take notes Listen for main ideas Listen and take detailed notes using a graphic organizer Relate listening to personal experiences and values Listen and take notes on listening Paraphrase main ideas of listening Classify sounds
Speaking Tasks:	Compare knowledge of and reactions to classical music Summarize information in an information gap activity Use figurative language in extemporaneous responses Pose and respond to questions using new vocabulary Role play an interview Use transitions to compare and contrast information Role play a school board meeting Conduct an experiment and report results
Pronunciation:	Joining final consonants
Vocabulary:	Context clues Synonyms Definitions Idiomatic expressions Vocabulary classification Figurative and literal usage
Grammar:	The passive voice and the passive causative

UNIT SUMMARY

This unit deals with research showing how the study of music and art in childhood can enhance intellectual performance. Listening One is a news report about the impressive results of two studies on the relationship between musical education and children's academic performance. Listening Two is an interview with a science journalist who discusses recent studies that reveal how music and art seem to strengthen areas of the brain.

The companion unit in *NorthStar: Reading and Writing* explores the role of art in one's life, particularly its healing qualities.

1 Focus on the Topic, PAGE 193

✪✪✪ A PREDICTING

Suggested Time: 5 minutes

Focus
To get students thinking about how the arts can enhance our intellectual performance.

Setup
Ask students to read the title and the cartoon and discuss the questions with a neighboring classmate. Have the pairs share their ideas with the class.

✪✪ B SHARING INFORMATION

Suggested Time: 20 minutes

Focus
To get students to listen to an excerpt of music and imagine how it could enhance one's abilities; to get students to discuss freely their experiences and schooling in the arts.

Setup
Have students listen to the music and write their own list of tasks before forming groups to compare lists and discuss the questions in Exercise 2. To enrich this discussion, have students from different fields of study work together.

Expansion/Homework
(1) As a class, you may want to elicit responses to Exercise 1 and write them on the board. Students may want to refer to these notes in the subsequent exercises to check the accuracy of their initial predictions. (2) Small groups of students could turn this section into a survey, recording each student's arts schooling and tallying the information for the class.

✪✪✪ C **PREPARING TO LISTEN**

BACKGROUND
Suggested Time: 25 minutes 🕐

Focus
To introduce students to terms used in scientific experiments; to get students to learn about and inform each other of three significant studies exploring the relationship between music and learning; to awaken interest in and aid comprehension of the listening that follows.

Setup
Have students read the text individually. Divide the class into groups of three. Assign each student in the group a different experiment to study. Have students read about their experiments, take notes, and then explain the experiment to the other members in their group. Then have them discuss the questions in Exercise 2. Ask the groups to share any reactions or insights with the class.

Expansion/Homework
(1) You could convert the reading into a listening exercise by reading the text aloud as students listen and take notes in the chart. (2) To encourage interaction as students explain their experiments, you can list phrases for clarifying and restating information (*In other words . . . /What you said was . . .*) and write them on the board for students' easy reference. (3) Instead of students explaining the experiments to each other, you can have students ask each other for the information. To prepare for this variation, brainstorm questions to ask for each topic using the prompts in the chart. Write the questions on the board for students' easy reference. (4) Encourage your students to follow this topic in the news or online. Have them bring any articles they find that mention art and music programs in schools to class.

VOCABULARY FOR COMPREHENSION
Suggested Time: 20 minutes 🕐

Focus
To familiarize students with vocabulary for discussing education and brain development; to acquaint students with vocabulary used to aid listening comprehension.

Setup
As a class, review the pronunciation of the underlined expressions in Exercise 1. Have students complete the exercise individually and then compare answers with a partner (someone from a different language background, if possible). Encourage students to consult each other and their dictionaries before consulting you. For Exercise 2, pair students of similar levels to match the definitions and words.

Expansion/Homework
(1) If class time is limited, you may want to assign both exercises as homework. In class, check answers and correct pronunciation. (2) If students struggle to

guess the meaning of the underlined words in Exercise 1, refer them to the list of definitions in Exercise 2. (3) To help students memorize vocabulary, have them work in pairs to quiz each other on the definitions in Exercise 2. One can play the teacher; the other can play the student. Then have them switch roles.

2 Focus on Listening, PAGE 198

✪✪✪A LISTENING ONE: *Does Music Enhance Math Skills?*
Suggested Time: 10 minutes ⏱

Focus
To get students to predict how music can strengthen math skills; to familiarize students with the tone of the speakers in the interview.

Setup
Have students work with a partner to list their ideas. To encourage use of the vocabulary learned in Section 1C, write the words on the board for students' reference. Have students listen to the excerpt and compare that list with their own. Ask students to share any reactions with the class.

Expansion/Homework
As a class, you may want to elicit ideas and write them on the board for students' reference after they listen to the excerpt.

✪✪✪ LISTENING FOR MAIN IDEAS
Suggested Time: 20 minutes ⏱

Focus
To help students listen for the main ideas in an extended news report and interview about the relationship between music and math.

Setup
Have students read the prompts before listening. Clarify any vocabulary. Play Parts One, Two, and Three, pausing after each part so students can complete their answers. Have students compare answers with a neighboring classmate. If disagreements arise, play each part again.

Expansion/Homework
To challenge more advanced students, convert this first listening into a note-taking activity. With books closed, have students take notes using a divided page: Main Ideas/Details. Then have students pair up with a neighboring classmate to compare notes. When finished, students can open their books and answer the questions using their notes.

✪✪✪ LISTENING FOR DETAILS
Suggested Time: 20 minutes ⏱

Focus
To get students to listen carefully again, this time for specific information.

Setup
Go over the chart carefully with the class. Play the interview, stopping it at times to let students compare answers. If disagreements arise, replay the part rather than give the answer. In some cases, students may even want to listen a third time.

✪✪ REACTING TO THE LISTENING
Suggested Time: 25 minutes ⏱

Focus
To encourage students to interpret information and make inferences about the interview; to encourage students to think and consider several possibilities in their responses.

Setup
Have students read the items before listening to the excerpts. Allow students a few minutes to think about how they would rank the items before discussing their judgments in small groups. If there is disagreement, welcome it. Encourage students to support their points of view with details from the interview. Emphasize that it is possible for students to have varying opinions, as long as their reasoning is sound. Have the groups report any especially interesting or insightful ideas they discussed to the class. For Exercise 2, have students form new groups (with students from different language backgrounds, if possible) to discuss the questions. Ask the groups to share with the class any interesting insights or ideas from their discussions.

Expansion/Homework
(1) As students discuss their opinions in Exercise 2, listen and note any errors on a divided page: Usage/Pronunciation. You can then distribute these notes to the groups of students. Have them return the papers to you with the usage errors corrected and the pronunciation words marked with stress marks over the stressed syllables. As a class, you can review the pronunciation of the most frequent errors. (2) Listen to the groups, noting the most interesting ideas. Present these on the board and invite comments. (3) Have students compose a final response to one of the questions in Exercise 2 and record it in their audio journals.

Link to *NorthStar: Reading and Writing*
You may want expand question 3 into a class discussion on the many levels on which music and the arts affect us. Ask, *In what other ways can music enrich us? How did it help in war-torn Sarajevo? How does it help people who are suffering? How can it enhance a person's self-expression?*

✪✪✪ B **LISTENING TWO:** *Music, Art, and the Brain*

Suggested Time: 20 minutes 🕐

Focus

To give students more information about the relationship between music and mathematical and analytical skills; to get students to practice their note-taking and summary skills.

Setup

To accentuate the difference between the two steps—note taking and summarizing—have students close their books as they listen to the interview to take notes. When the excerpt is finished, allow them to open their books, write their summaries, and compare with a partner.

Expansion/Homework

(1) Model the first part with the class before you ask students to work with partners. (2) At the end of this interview, the scientist editor suggested ways to boost your child's intelligence. Ask students, *If/when you have children, would you use anything you have learned from these listenings to boost your child's intelligence? Why? Why not?*

✪✪✪ C **LINKING LISTENINGS ONE AND TWO**

Suggested Time: 25 minutes 🕐

Focus

To get students to synthesize and integrate what they have learned in the listening in a simulation activity.

Setup

Have students work in groups of three to evaluate the proposals. Encourage students to review their notes and the transcripts of the interviews. Set a time limit of 15 minutes for these group discussions. Then have each group, with one student from each group acting as the candidate, present its single proposal to the class. Pull the candidate aside for a moment to discuss his/her criteria (for example, feasibility and cost).

Expansion/Homework

(1) Before beginning this section, you may want to have students orally restate each experiment in pairs, small groups, or as a class, to help strengthen their overall grasp of the material. (2) Students could prepare an audio journal response to the question, *Why should the [local] elementary school keep its arts program in a time of financial crisis?*

3 Focus on Vocabulary, PAGE 203

✪ EXERCISE 1
Suggested Time: 25 minutes ◷

Focus
To expand and reinforce unit vocabulary; to get students to distinguish between the figurative and literal meanings of certain words.

Setup
Introduce the concept of *literal* and *figurative*, using the example sentence. Have students work in pairs to complete Exercise 1. You may want to go over the answers from the Answer Key with the class.

Expansion/Homework
(1) Exercise 1 can be converted into a listening exercise by having pairs of students take turns reading the sentences aloud. The student who listens must decide whether the word is used figuratively or literally. (2) Or, if class time is limited, you could assign this exercise for homework. (3) You may want to invite students to come up with their own pairs of figurative and literal words to present to the class, or give them an additional list and have them come up with the two meanings and write contextualized sentences.

✪ EXERCISE 2
Suggested Time: 25 minutes ◷

Focus
To practice using the unit vocabulary in a guided conversation.

Setup
Have students work in pairs (with students from different language backgrounds, if possible) to ask and answer the questions. When students finish the first part, have them switch roles.

✪ EXERCISE 3
Suggested Time: 30 minutes ◷

Focus
To give students additional practice defining and using the vocabulary in this unit.

Setup
Have students work with a partner (someone from a different language background, if possible) to complete the exercise. Go over the answers aloud to check pronunciation.

Expansion/Homework
(1) This exercise can be converted into a listening exercise by having pairs of students take turns reading the sentences aloud. The student who listens must identify the synonym. (2) For further practice of this vocabulary, students could

write a brief history of their study of English from the first time they uttered an English word to today, using as many of these vocabulary items as possible. (3) To help students memorize vocabulary, have them work in pairs to quiz each other on the definitions. One can play the teacher; the other can play the student. Then have them switch roles.

✪ EXERCISE 4
Suggested Time: 30 minutes 🕐

Focus
To give a playful approach to the use of unit vocabulary.

Setup
Model the game for the whole class. Have students of similar ages form groups to set up the game. Then call out a start time. Monitor teamwork to ensure students are focused on the prompts and not just running through a list of responses to find the right word. Award the winning team with applause. Then have the teams play again.

Expansion/Homework
When playing the word game, students can use prompts other than questions, for example, omitting the word from the sentence and having the team fill it in, using the word in the question so that it is repeated in the response, or having the whole team create a story using the words on the board.

 For extra vocabulary practice, have students work on the self-grading vocabulary activities for the unit on the NorthStar Companion Website at **http://www.longman.com/northstar**.

4 Focus on Speaking, PAGE 209

✪✪ A │ PRONUNCIATION: Joining Final Consonants
Suggested Time: 25 minutes 🕐

Focus
To identify how sounds in words link together in speech and to practice linking expressions and phrases from this unit.

Setup
Read the introductory passage aloud or have students read it silently. Instead of playing the audio in Exercise 1, you may want to demonstrate the examples yourself. Have students work in pairs (with students from different language backgrounds, if possible) to practice pronouncing these phrases. For Exercise 2, review the pronunciation of the phrases by playing the audio or modeling them yourself. Have students code the phrases before they complete the sentences.

Have students compare their answers with a partner. Call on individual students to read the sentence aloud to check pronunciation.

Expansion/Homework
You could have students code the phrases in Exercise 1 and then compare their markings in pairs.

✪✪B GRAMMAR: The Passive Voice and the Passive Causative
Suggested Time: 25 minutes ⏲

Focus
To get students to understand how to form the passive voice, when to use it, and how it differs from the passive causative; to add interest to the topic with a study on the influence of piano lessons on a child's spatial reasoning; to provide practice of the grammar point in a guided conversation.

Setup
Have the class study the examples in Exercise 1 and answer the two questions that follow. Ask students to read the grammar explanations silently. Have students complete Exercise 2 individually. Review answers orally to work on pronunciation. Check comprehension by asking, *According to this study, can children learn more from a computer keyboard or a piano keyboard? Why?* In Exercise 3, have students from different cultural backgrounds work together to perform the role play. Allow them a few minutes to prepare before they begin. To encourage a conversational tone in this exercise, have students read the information in the book silently and then look at their partners to speak. They may need to break the information into smaller pieces to retell it. It doesn't matter how frequently they refer to the book as long as they are looking at their partners when they speak.

Expansion/Homework
(1) If class time is limited, Exercises 1 and 2 may be assigned as homework.
(2) You may want to have students write several passive sentences using the information in the chart on page 211. You can create an error-correction exercise from sentences in which students misuse the passive. Students may also contrast the stylistic effects of passive voice and active voice by transforming some of the sentences from one to the other. (3) You may want to mention the verbs in English that don't take the passive form: *appear, consist of, collide, disappear, emerge, happen, last, look, occur, resemble, seem, take place, vanish,* and *weigh.* (4) For further practice, offer exercises from *Focus on Grammar, Advanced* and from Azar's *Understanding and Using English Grammar.* See the Grammar Book References on page 248 of the Student Book.

✪✪✪C STYLE: Expressions That Link Sentences or Ideas
Suggested Time: 25 minutes ⏲

Focus
To get students to practice using expressions of comparison and contrast; to compare and contrast concepts presented in this unit.

Setup

Have students read the examples silently. Model the phrases and have students repeat them until they are confident of their own pronunciation and intonation. Pair stronger and weaker students together to do the exercise. Allow them a few minutes to read through the whole chart, while you write the phrases on the board for easy reference.

Expansion/Homework

The exercise could be assigned for homework, by having students write their sentences. Class time can be used to compare the sentences in small groups.

 For extra listening practice, have students use the NorthStar Companion Video.

✪✪✪ D   SPEAKING TOPIC

Focus

To integrate the concepts, vocabulary, pronunciation skills (joining final consonants), grammar (the passive voice and the passive causative), and style focus (expressions that link sentences or ideas) of the unit; to illustrate how research affects practice in the United States; to conduct a meeting on the proposed elimination of art and music classes from an elementary school curriculum.

Setup

Have students read the background and the case study. Check comprehension. Ask, *What is a school board? How are schools funded? What areas have already been proposed for cuts? How has the community reacted to the proposed art and music cuts?* Have students form three groups: parents, teachers, and school board members, and one student volunteer to chair the meeting. Have each group read its role description and write its position on the issue. Meanwhile, with the "leader," brainstorm phrases for opening, conducting, and closing a meeting.

Expansion/Homework

(1) You may want to write expressions from Sections 1C (Vocabulary for Comprehension) and 3 (Focus on Vocabulary) on small pieces of paper and distribute them to students. As they speak, they must try to incorporate their assigned phrases. (2) During the meeting, note the most salient usage and pronunciation errors. You can then distribute these notes to the individual students. Have them correct the usage errors and mark the pronunciation words with stress marks over the stressed syllables. Then have them share their corrections with a partner (someone from a different language background, if possible) so they gain feedback. Circulate around the room answering students' questions. As a class, you can review the pronunciation of the most frequent errors. (3) After the meeting, have students reflect on the situation.

Emphasize that education in the United States is controlled locally, so this is an authentic situation.

⊛E   RESEARCH TOPIC

Focus
To conduct an experiment on the influence of Mozart's music on intellectual performance; to have fun testing the hypothesis presented in the unit.

Setup
Have the class assign the roles and then conduct the experiment.

Expansion/Homework
(1) You might want to have students try different kinds of music to see how it influences their performance. (2) For further reading on this topic, the following text is recommended: *The Mozart Effect: Tapping the Power of Music to Heal the Body, Strengthen the Mind, and Unlock the Creative Spirit,* by Don Campbell.

Link to *NorthStar: Reading and Writing*
If time allows, you could do a speaking topic from Section 4D (in class) and a writing topic (at home). You will probably want to choose the research topic that fits your students and the classroom environment best. When students speak, remind them to use vocabulary and examples from the Reading/Writing material on the healing qualities of art.

Television and Freedom of Expression

OVERVIEW	
Theme:	First Amendment Issues

Listenings:	Listening One: *Interview with* Newsweek *Entertainment Editor*
	    A radio interview
	Listening Two: *Interview with Former Chairman of MPAA*
	    Ratings Board
	    A radio interview

Critical Thinking Skills:	Hypothesize outcomes Recognize personal biases and assumptions about the media Evaluate a ratings system Identify and defend points of view in a text Make informed judgments using interview information Develop arguments for or against an issue Define a problem and propose a solution
Listening Tasks:	Identify the main ideas Listen for details Interpret speaker's intent by analyzing tone and word usage Relate listening to personal experiences and values Listen for supporting ideas in an argument Synthesize information in two listenings Listen for word stress in speech Interview and take notes on interviewees' responses
Speaking Tasks:	Make predictions Support an opinion with examples and reasoning Use new vocabulary in a role play Use phrasal verbs in extemporaneous responses Express varying degrees of certainty with modals Express doubts or reservations Debate the issue of freedom of speech Interview people and summarize findings
Pronunciation:	Word stress of phrasal verbs
Vocabulary:	Context clues Synonyms and word definitions Idiomatic expressions Phrasal verbs
Grammar:	Modals—degrees of certainty

UNIT SUMMARY

This unit deals with the use of the V-chip (violence chip) as a means of censoring violence, sex, and vulgar language on television. Listening One is an interview with a supporter of the V-chip and the TV ratings system. Listening Two is an interview with an opponent of the V-chip technology who seeks nonvoluntary regulation that would discourage the amount of violence, sex, and vulgarity in the TV industry.

The companion unit in *NorthStar: Reading and Writing* explores book banning and the ways in which freedom of speech has been threatened in the United States.

1 Focus on the Topic, PAGE 219

✪✪✪ A PREDICTING

Suggested Time: 10 minutes ⏱

Focus
To get students thinking about violence on TV and its influence on children.

Setup
Ask students to read the title and cartoon, and discuss the questions in a small group. Have the groups share their ideas with the class.

Expansion/Homework
As a class, you may want to elicit responses and write them on the board.

✪✪ B SHARING INFORMATION

Suggested Time: 30 minutes ⏱

Focus
To introduce students to the TV and movie ratings systems used in the United States; to get students to discuss freely their opinions on ratings systems and issues of freedom of speech.

Setup
Before the class reads this material, point out that these ratings systems are under development and are constantly changing. Have students read Rating Movies (page 220) before forming groups to discuss the questions in Exercise 1. To enrich this discussion, have students of different ages work together.

Expansion/Homework
You could lead a class discussion about ratings systems in different countries. Ask students, *How are movies rated in other countries? What is considered obscene in other countries?*

✿✿✿ C **PREPARING TO LISTEN**

BACKGROUND
Suggested Time: 20 minutes 🕑

Focus
To introduce students to the complex issue of how to control the level of violence portrayed on TV without the government censoring content; to get students to identify different groups' viewpoints on the issue and summarize their positions.

Setup
Have students read the text individually. Check comprehension by asking, *Why do people oppose government regulation of TV violence?* Then have students of varying ages work in small groups to identify the source of each statement.

Expansion/Homework
(1) You may want to assign the reading as homework. Then students can discuss their opinions as a class. (2) You could convert this into a listening exercise by reading the text aloud as students listen. Check their comprehension with the question in Setup. (3) You could read the quotations aloud. As students listen, they can identify the speakers. If there is disagreement, repeat the quotation. (4) To engage the students more immediately in the categorization, photocopy the quotations on separate cards and then have students sort them into four piles (USG, TI, P, FSS). (5) Encourage your students to follow this topic in the news or online. Have them bring to class any articles they find that mention ratings systems or censorship of TV or movies.

VOCABULARY FOR COMPREHENSION
Suggested Time: 10 minutes 🕑

Focus
To familiarize students with vocabulary used to discuss TV and movie ratings; to acquaint students with vocabulary to aid listening comprehension.

Setup
Go over the pronunciation of the underlined words. Ask students to work individually to complete the exercise. As students finish, have them pair up to compare answers. If disagreements arise, encourage them to consult each other and their dictionaries before consulting you.

Expansion/Homework
(1) If class time is limited, you may want to assign this section as homework. In class, check answers and work on pronunciation. (2) To help students memorize vocabulary, have them work in pairs to quiz each other on the definitions. One can play the teacher; the other can play the student. Then they switch roles.

2 Focus on Listening, PAGE 223

✪✪✪ A **LISTENING ONE:** *Interview with* Newsweek *Entertainment Editor*

Suggested Time: 10 minutes ⏱

Focus
To get students to predict the content of the interview.

Setup
In pairs, have students listen to the beginning of the interview and then write three questions they expect to hear answered. Encourage them to use the vocabulary from Section 1C by writing the list of words on the board.

Expansion/Homework
You could elicit students' questions as a class, writing them on the board. If, after the interview, some of the students' questions remain unanswered, ask them to imagine how Rick Marin might have responded.

✪✪✪ **LISTENING FOR MAIN IDEAS**

Suggested Time: 20 minutes ⏱

Focus
To help students listen for the main ideas in an extended interview on TV ratings.

Setup
Have students read the questions before listening. Clarify any vocabulary. Play Parts One, Two, and Three, pausing after each part so students can complete their writing. Have students compare answers with a neighboring classmate. If disagreements arise, play each part again.

Expansion/Homework
To challenge more advanced students, convert Listening One into a note-taking activity. With books closed, have students take notes on a divided page: Main Ideas/ Details. Then have students pair up with a neighboring classmate to compare notes. When finished, students can open their books and answer the questions.

✪✪✪ **LISTENING FOR DETAILS**

Suggested Time: 20 minutes ⏱

Focus
To get students to listen carefully again, this time for specific pieces of information.

Setup
First have students read the true/false statements and answer the ones they already know. Play the interview again. As students listen, have them evaluate and correct the statements. Have them compare their answers with a neighboring classmate. If disagreements arise, replay the segment rather than give the answer.

Expansion/Homework

(1) Each student can compose an additional true/false statement to present to the class. (2) You can convert this comprehension exercise into a listening activity by reading the true/false statements aloud to the class and inviting students to react. Encourage students to support their opinions with information from the listening. You may need to replay parts of the interview for clarification.

✪✪ REACTING TO THE LISTENING
Suggested Time: 25 minutes ⏱

Focus

To encourage students to interpret tone of voice and word choice to determine a speaker's intention; to encourage students to consider several possibilities in their responses; to promote critical discussion of and reflection on the interview.

Setup

Have students read the questions before listening to the excerpts. Allow students a few minutes to think about their responses before sharing them with a partner and then with the class. If there is disagreement, welcome it. Encourage students to support their points of view with details from the interview. To enrich this discussion, try to pair students of varying backgrounds and ages. With their same partners, have students discuss the questions in Exercise 2.

Expansion/Homework

(1) To help strengthen students' overall grasp of the material, you may want to divide them into the five constituent groups (the government; parents; the TV industry; teenagers; and free-speech supporters) to summarize the group's position and present it to the class. (2) You may want to refer to the cartoon on page 219 and ask students, *What does this cartoon say about the "forbidden fruit" concept?* (3) For homework, students could respond to one of the questions in Exercise 2 in their audio journals.

✪✪✪ B   LISTENING TWO: *Interview with Former Chairman of MPAA Ratings Board*
Suggested Time: 30 minutes ⏱

Focus

To give students a different perspective on the controversy of TV ratings; to expose students to a different and highly opinionated speaker.

Setup

Go over the statements with the class. Have students check them off as they listen to the interview. Play the interview several times so students are certain they checked all the relevant items.

Expansion/Homework

You may want students to read the statements and predict how Richard Heffner would respond.

✪✪✪C **LINKING LISTENINGS ONE AND TWO**
Suggested Time: 15 minutes ⏲

Focus

To get students to remember and interpret information from the two interviews; to get students to develop, express, and defend their opinions using supporting details from the interviews.

Setup

Have students read the statements and register their opinions individually. Then have pairs of students from different language backgrounds discuss their opinions. You can write on the board expressions for discussing opinions from the Style section of Unit 2 (page 42) for students' reference as they speak. Ask the pairs to share any interesting insights or ideas from their discussion.

Expansion/Homework

(1) If class time is limited, you could assign the first part of this exercise as homework. (2) As students discuss their opinions, listen and note any errors on a divided page: Usage/Pronunciation. You can then distribute these notes to the pairs of students. Have them return the papers to you with the usage errors corrected and the pronunciation words marked with stress marks over the stressed syllables. As a class you can review the pronunciation of the most frequent errors. (3) Encourage students to bring any articles that are relevant to this topic to class and be ready to summarize them.

Link to *NorthStar: Reading and Writing*

Ask, *What point of view would Marcia Cohen have on TV ratings and censorship technology? How is the use of this technology similar to book banning? How is it different? Do you think it is possible for a parent to oppose book banning and support censorship technology? Is that position hypocritical?*

3 Focus on Vocabulary, PAGE 228

✪ **EXERCISE 1**
Suggested Time: 15 minutes ⏲

Focus

To give students more practice defining and using the vocabulary in this unit.

Setup

As a class, practice pronouncing the new vocabulary. Have students work individually to complete the exercise, and then compare answers in pairs.

Expansion/Homework

To give further practice of the vocabulary in this unit, have students use at least five of the expressions from this section to write a paragraph about a television show they have watched.

✪ **EXERCISE 2**
   Suggested Time: 15 minutes 🕒

   ### Focus
   To use unit vocabulary as students review the issue of free speech and censorship.

   ### Setup
   As a class, practice pronouncing the new vocabulary. Have students read the whole article before filling in the blanks. Review answers as a class, correcting students' pronunciation.

   ### Expansion/Homework
   Students can first complete the article in their own words, treating it as a cloze exercise.

✪ **EXERCISE 3**
   Suggested Time: 20 minutes 🕒

   ### Focus
   To use unit vocabulary in a guided conversation about television censorship, reviewing the divergent points of view on this controversial issue.

   ### Setup
   Give students a few minutes of preparation time to take notes before they ask and answer the questions using the vocabulary listed. To encourage the conversational tone of these exercises, have students read the information in the book silently and then look up at their partners to speak. It doesn't matter how frequently they refer to the book as long as they are looking at their partner when they speak. Make sure students switch roles after question 3.

 For extra vocabulary practice, have students work on the self-grading vocabulary activities for the unit on the NorthStar Companion Website at **http://www.longman.com/northstar**.

4 Focus on Speaking, PAGE 231

✪✪ **A** **PRONUNCIATION: Word Stress of Phrasal Verbs**
   Suggested Time: 20 minutes 🕒

   ### Focus
   To get students to recognize and produce the stress patterns of phrasal verbs; to review information on media, communications, and ratings systems.

Setup

Have students read the examples and the explanation. Read the examples aloud. In Exercise 1, play the audio and have students listen and mark the stressed words. Then have them work in pairs to compare answers and practice pronouncing the verbs. With the same partners, have them take turns asking and answering the questions in Exercise 2, using the phrasal verbs listed. If necessary, they may check answers in small groups, or you can provide them with the answers from the Answer Key.

Expansion/Homework

You may want to invite groups of students to brainstorm a list of other phrasal verbs to present to the class.

✪✪B GRAMMAR: Modals—Degrees of Certainty

Suggested Time: 25 minutes 🔊

Focus

To get students to understand how to form and use the various modals that indicate degrees of certainty; to use modals to discuss opinions about violence, the media, and ratings systems.

Setup

Have the class study the examples in Exercise 1 and answer the two questions that follow. Ask students to read the grammar explanations silently. Have students work in pairs to take turns asking and answering the questions in Exercise 2. Encourage them to add their own opinions. Have students change partners and complete Exercise 3. To encourage the conversational tone of these exercises, have students read the information in the book silently and then look at their partners to speak. It doesn't matter how frequently they refer to the book as long as they are looking at their partner when they speak.

Expansion/Homework

(1) If possible, have students record these exchanges. They can listen for pronunciation and usage errors, which they can write down and then correct. (2) If taping is not possible, circulate around the room, listening to the students. Take notes on their pronunciation and usage. When they are finished with the speaking activity, write the usage errors on the board (or on a transparency for the overhead projector) and invite students to correct the errors. For pronunciation correction, write the words to be practiced on the board, invite the class to identify the stressed syllables, model the pronunciation, and encourage students to practice repeating the words or phrases until they are confident of their own pronunciation. (3) Have each pair stand in front of the class and deliver a dramatic exchange modeled on one of these exercises. (4) For further practice, offer exercises from *Focus on Grammar, Advanced* and from Azar's *Understanding and Using English Grammar*. See the Grammar Book References on page 248 of the Student Book.

✪✪✪ C | **STYLE: Expressing Doubts or Reservations**

Suggested Time: 25 minutes

Focus
To get students to practice expressing doubts or reservations while discussing the information in this unit.

Setup
Have students read the examples silently. Model the phrases and have students repeat them until they are confident of their own pronunciation and intonation. Point out that students can also couple these expressions with the modal form (Section 4B) to express uncertainty. Pair stronger and weaker students together to do the exercise.

Expansion/Homework
(1) After students work in pairs, you could give them further practice by reading aloud the strong viewpoints presented in the exercise and inviting students to respond to the statements with caution and reservation. (2) You may want to brainstorm more phrases for expressing uncertainty, for example: *I have mixed feelings about that./I'm not 100% sure./That's a gray area*. These can be written on the board for students' reference while they speak.

For extra listening practice, have students use the NorthStar Companion Video.

✪✪✪ D | **SPEAKING TOPIC**

Focus
To integrate the concepts, vocabulary, pronunciation skills (word stress of phrasal verbs), grammar (modals: degrees of certainty), and style focus (expressing doubts or reservations) of the unit to conduct a debate on the Telecommunications Law.

Setup
Divide the class into two teams: for and against the Telecommunications Law. Give the teams at least 15 minutes to develop their arguments. Meanwhile, write the phrases for framing an argument from the Style section of Unit 7 (page 164) on the board for students' reference. During the debate, you can play the role of impartial timekeeper and protocol enforcer. The teams take timed turns offering opening statements, position points, rebuttals, and conclusions. Conduct a debriefing session after the debate to hear students' reactions to the case. Have students write the letter in Exercise 4 as a homework assignment.

Expansion/Homework
(1) Have students reflect on the quality of their debate. Encourage them to appreciate their efforts and their language. (2) During the meeting, take notes of the most salient usage and pronunciation errors. After the debate, you can distribute these notes to the individual students. Have them correct the usage errors and mark the pronunciation words with stress marks over the stressed

syllables. Circulate around the room answering students' questions. As a class, you can review the pronunciation of the most frequent errors. (3) Students can form small groups to read their letters aloud. Encourage them to give each other feedback on the arguments presented.

✪E   RESEARCH TOPIC

Focus
To conduct several brief interviews on the topic of the V-chip and TV ratings; to practice reporting skills.

Setup
Have students work with partners of their own choosing to develop questions for their interviews. Have them go to a public area to conduct their interviews so that they may encounter a broad cross-section of the population. Have the pairs report their findings to the class. Then conduct a debriefing of their experiences as roving reporters.

Expansion/Homework
For further reading on this topic, the following texts are recommended: *The First Amendment: Freedom of Speech, Religion, and the Press*, by Leah Farish; and *Abandoned in the Wasteland: Children, Television and the First Amendment*, by Newton N. Minow.

Link to *NorthStar: Reading and Writing*
If time allows, you could do a writing topic from Section 4C (at home) and a speaking topic (in class). You will probably want to choose the research topic that fits your students and the environment best. When students speak, remind them to use examples and vocabulary from the Reading/Writing unit on book banning.

Student Book Answer Key

UNIT 1

VOCABULARY FOR COMPREHENSION, page 4

1. i	5. h	8. a	11. g
2. d	6. b	9. j	12. m
3. k	7. c	10. f	13. e
4. l			

LISTENING FOR MAIN IDEAS, page 5

Kandell's view of Internet addiction: It is not a new addiction. Some people may have been addicted for a while. Internet use is more widespread now, so Internet addiction is growing, especially on college campuses.

Chief symptoms/warning signs of Internet addiction: When too much Internet use begins to affect other parts of students' lives.

Possible treatment: Support group for Internet addiction.

LISTENING FOR DETAILS, page 5

Examples of addictions: gambling, sex, shopping, video games, on-line chat rooms.

Evidence for this view: Students are coming to Kandell more often for help with relationship problems or problems with their grades, but the real problem is not relationships or grades but rather their overuse of the Net.

Other symptoms/warning signs: When computer use affects work performance or school performance or relationships; when students start losing some of the skills that make relationships successful; when friends begin to comment on Internet overuse.

Reasons this treatment is helpful: Students have a chance to talk and deal with people face to face; they leave the isolation of the their room; they help each other strategize on the best way to break the pattern and figure out what is causing these problems.

REACTING TO THE LISTENING

1 page 6

Excerpt One

By using the word "groupies," he wants to attract the attention of a particular group in the audience—people who are technology enthusiasts. The word implies that Internet enthusiasts "follow" the technology trend of using the Internet, just as music enthusiasts ("groupies") follow popular singers or bands.

Excerpt Two

"Well . . . uh . . . I mean . . . for some people . . ." He doesn't seem to want to make a firm statement that Internet addiction is a definite problem on college campuses. That would be a very controversial stance for a psychologist, and he would most likely need more scientific and medical proof. Instead, he is tentative and gives an anecdotal observation that "they" are seeing more cases of kids being addicted.

Excerpt Three

He is skeptical and a little cynical. He addresses Kandell very informally and almost jokingly. He says amusingly, imitating a student, "Doc, you gotta help me!" This implies that he is taking the topic less seriously than he could be *or* that he is imitating the informality of college students' speech in order to be funny.

B LISTENING TWO

1 page 7

MAIN IDEAS

Advantage of multitasking:

It makes the brain work better and faster.

General view of creativity and how it occurs:

Creativity happens slowly when the brain is just noodling around or playing.

Effect of technology on Brooks:

His way of thinking is negatively affected. He is also addicted to new technology.

DETAILS

Reasons for his attitude:

New technology creates more communication and we become overwhelmed with information.

Additional advantages of multitasking:

Certain skills are enhanced, such as the ability to make fast decisions, to answer many e-mails in a short period of time, to do certain standardized tests like the SAT.

Specific ways to enhance creativity:

Creativity happens when you put together unrelated ideas—for example, when you take time to read a book about history or philosophy and relate the ideas you read about to your own business or life.

Examples of effect on Brooks:

Even when he is supposed to be relaxing, he is thinking about his voice mail or answering his cell phones.

2 page 7

1. T
2. T
3. F (It limits creativity.)
4. F (You should read things outside the field of business such as history or philosophy.)
5. F (You should not answer every e-mail immediately. You should take time to read unrelated things and let your mind play with ideas.)
6. T

3 FOCUS ON VOCABULARY

1 page 10

NOUN	VERB	ADJECTIVE
1. addict 2. addiction	X	1. addicted 2. addictive
anxiety	X	anxious
1. compulsiveness 2. compulsion	X	compulsive
depression	depress	1. depressed 2. depressive
enhancement	enhance	enhanced
fulfillment	fulfill	1. fulfilling 2. fulfilled
isolation	isolate	isolated
X	overwhelm	1. overwhelmed 2. overwhelming
problem	X	problematic
strategy	strategize	strategic
support	support	1. supportive 2. supporting
symptom	X	symptomatic
therapy	X	therapeutic

2 page 11

1. compulsive
2. overwhelmed
3. problematic
4. anxiety
5. symptoms
6. fulfilled
7. depressed
8. strategies
9. addicted
10. isolating
11. supportive
12. therapeutic

4 page 12

1. f	4. d	7. h	10. j
2. k	5. b	8. a	11. l
3. c	6. e	9. i	12. g

A PRONUNCIATION

1 page 14

1. Patty was running up <u>huge</u> sums of money on her credit cards.
2. She spent <u>thousands</u> of dollars.
3. <u>Nothing</u> could stop her.
4. She was <u>totally</u> out of control.
5. <u>Fifteen</u> cups of coffee a day was the <u>only</u> thing that kept Jim going.

6. <u>Totally</u> overwhelmed by work, he drank from <u>5</u> in the morning to 11 at night.
7. Now, addicted to both coffee <u>and</u> the Internet, his life was a <u>complete</u> disaster.
8. He couldn't get to a therapist's office <u>fast</u> enough.

2 page 15

A: Workaholism isn't <u>really</u> an addiction. Some people have <u>no</u> choice <u>but</u> to work <u>long</u> hours.
B: Not <u>only</u> that. A <u>lot</u> of people are workaholics because they <u>love</u> what they do.
A: <u>Agreed</u>, but being <u>driven</u> to succeed at all costs may not be such a good thing.
B: Yeah, that makes me think of my father. He was <u>so</u> hooked on work, he used to <u>drive</u> talking on his cell phone and checking his <u>e-mail</u> at red lights.
A: You <u>must</u> be joking. That is multi<u>tasking</u> at its <u>best</u>!
B: Well, not <u>exactly</u>. He just lost his <u>driver's</u> license after getting into his <u>third</u> accident and getting his <u>fifth</u> ticket.

UNIT 2

BACKGROUND, page 26

Religion: Plymouth, Brook Farm

Community: Brook Farm, Hippie Communies, New Urbanist Communities

Environment: Brook Farm, Hippie Communes, New Urbanist Communities

Education: New Harmony, Brook Farm

VOCABULARY FOR COMPREHENSION, page 27

a. 6	f. 11	k. 12
b. 8	g. 10	l. 13
c. 5	h. 14	m. 15
d. 2	i. 4	n. 3
e. 1	j. 7	o. 9

LISTENING FOR MAIN IDEAS, page 28

1. No, he wouldn't agree with this. The movie, *The Truman Show,* was set in Seaside, another example of a New Urbanist town like Celebration.
2. Yes, he would agree. Celebration has very expensive homes situated next to more moderately priced apartments.
3. Yes, he would agree. The residents were scrutinized by the media.
4. No, he wouldn't agree. Residents settled in Celebration to escape typical suburban life, not urban life.
5. No, he wouldn't agree. Ross was more interested in Celebration's social rather than physical landscape.

6. No, he wouldn't agree. Celebration will not be able to attract low-income residents because housing is getting too expensive.

LISTENING FOR DETAILS, page 29

1. F
2. F (Seaside, Florida, is a real town. It was the setting for a movie, but not a Disney movie.)
3. T
4. T
5. F (The residents felt uncomfortable speaking to the media because there was too much attention paid to them.)
6. T
7. T
8. F (The residents chose to live there themselves.)
9. F (In the beginning they did, but then they felt there was *too much* community.)
10. F (He is going back to visit.)

REACTING TO THE LISTENING

1 page 30
Suggested answers:

Excerpt One

1. He might feel that Seaside is really not such a nice place to live. It "looked like" a nice place in the movie.

Excerpt Two

2. Most likely, he is sympathetic to them. He conveys his sympathy with strong words and expressions such as "most scrutinized people on the planet," and "very high level of performance anxiety," and "ceaselessly assessing."

3. He might use words such as "examined, reported on" instead of "most scrutinized"; "nervousness" instead of "anxiety"; "checking on" instead of "ceaselessly assessing."

Excerpt Three

4. Perhaps he feels disappointed that low-income folks can't afford to live there. He refers to the "working people" he knew as "pioneers," which implies he admired them. Saying "Lord knows how they made ends meet" also implies he was respectfully surprised by how the low income folks could manage in the town.

Excerpt Four

5. It could be that the interviewer thought Ross's year in Celebration was "unreal." He emphasizes the words "back in your life" as if his year in Celebration were not real. Brancaccio might feel Manhattan is not a very warm or friendly city. He uses the words "callous" and "sophisticated" to refer to Ross's friends in Manhattan.

B LISTENING TWO, page 32

DETAILS

Design elements: small-town America

- houses close together
- sidewalks
- front porches
- tree-lined streets
- access to town on foot
- houses surround open areas
- lots of big parks and common areas

Physical design: social implications

- people out on porches and talking to their neighbors
- people walking down the streets and riding their bikes

Reality: "front-porch culture"

- too hot; people indoors in air-conditioning, not out on porches

Collins's attitude toward rules

- likes to break them
- sometimes silly, sometimes not

Frantz's attitude toward rules

- some rules may go too far
- reason for the rules; if you chose to live in Celebration, you should live by the rules

3 FOCUS ON VOCABULARY

1 page 34

2. c (*Callous* is a common characterization of people who live in Manhattan, and *idealistic* is a common characterization of Disneyphiles in Celebration.)
3. b (Scrutiny can cause performance anxiety in the same way that overwork can produce burnout.)
4. b (We live by or follow rules in the same way we obey or follow principles.)
5. c (The Disney planners wanted to create a town that generated nostalgia just as George Ripley of Brook Farm sought to generate spirituality in his utopia.)
6. b (Front-porch culture is an icon of small-town America just as Mickey Mouse is an icon of Disney World.)
7. a (*Vibrant* is a synonym for *energetic* just as *thwarted* is a synonym for *prevented*.)
8. a (*Envision* is similar in meaning to *imagine* just as *engineer* is similar in meaning to *create*.)

2 page 36

1. c	5. i	9. k	13. p
2. j	6. f	10. n	14. l
3. e	7. h	11. a	15. d
4. o	8. g	12. m	16. b

A PRONUNCIATION

1 page 38

1. **b.** lunch is
   c. lunches
   d. lunch has

2. **a.** porches
   b. porch is
   c. porch has
   d. porch as

3. **a.** house has
   b. house is
   c. house as
   d. houses

4. **a.** garages
   b. garage is
   c. garage has
   d. garage as

2 page 39

1. b
2. c
3. d
4. e
5. a

B GRAMMAR

2 page 41

2. He recommended that future residents live by the rules or not move to Celebration.
3. They might insist that the company hire a new school principal.
4. It is essential that journalists respect the residents' desire to avoid media scrutiny.
5. *Answers will vary.*
6. They'll recommend that less pricey houses be built.
7. They said it was essential that the Disney Corporation achieve racial and economic diversity.
8. They were demanding that the new mega supermarket not be built downtown.
9. It is critical that Celebration be free from crime, grime, and traffic.
10. *Answers will vary.*

UNIT 3

VOCABULARY FOR COMPREHENSION

2 page 51

1. f	4. h	7. l	10. e
2. c	5. d	8. i	11. b
3. j	6. a	9. g	12. k

LISTENING FOR MAIN IDEAS, page 52

Part One

1. Forty-eight percent of Americans label themselves as shy, and the number is growing.

2. **Cultural factors:** competition, testing, emphasis on individual merit
   Social factors: electronic revolution isolates people, smaller families, fewer extended families that give children the opportunity to learn social interaction skills

Part Two

3. **Situational shyness:** momentary shyness based on the situation
   Dispositional shyness: chronic shyness that exists regardless of the situation

4. Shy people should admit their shyness.

5. People make false assumptions that they are aloof or condescending. Rather, they are simply shy.

LISTENING FOR DETAILS

1 page 53

Part One	Part Two
1. a	7. c
2. c	8. c
3. a	9. b
4. c	10. b
5. a	11. a
6. a	12. b

REACTING TO THE LISTENING

1 page 53

Excerpt One

1. He is ironically telling the radio listeners not to worry. He uses the word *friends* to create a sort of mock intimacy between him and the audience before approaching the rather personal topic of shyness.

2. He is making fun of the topic and doesn't really take it too seriously.

Excerpt Two

3. He places stress on the word *amazement.* He also paraphrases his data to indicate his emphasis on the research.

Excerpt Three

4. He might feel a bit embarrassed initially by the question. First, we hear a hesitation in his voice; but then, we hear a smile in his tone of voice once he starts to explain.

B LISTENING TWO

1 page 56

1. c	4. b
2. e	5. d
3. a	

3 FOCUS ON VOCABULARY

1 page 58

1. virtually
2. outlook
3. take things as
4. widespread
5. In the first place
6. mark
7. think of
8. wind up
9. drawing out
10. fill the void
11. break the ice

3 page 60

Introvert

bashful / inhibited / petrified / reserved / reticent / self-conscious / shrinking violet / standoffish / timid / wallflower

Extrovert

assertive / bold / gregarious / life of the party / open / outgoing / sociable / social butterfly / talk a blue streak

Pessimist

gloomy / killjoy / negative / whiny

Optimist

open / Pollyanna / positive / upbeat

A PRONUNCIATION

1 page 62

1. We discovered that about 40 percent of all Americans label themselves as shy.
2. Over the past ten years, that figure has increased to about 48 percent.
3. Do you find these days that it's more difficult meeting people?
4. Two out of every five people you meet think of themselves as shy.
5. There are many just things in a culture, our culture, which lead lots of people to be shy.
6. Children don't see . . . don't have the opportunity to see their parents and relatives relating in a natural, easy, friendly way.
7. When you're at a party, or just in a conversation with someone anywhere and you recognize that they're shy, what do you do to draw them out or try to make them more comfortable?
8. Admitting your shyness is really an important first step because if you don't, people make misattributions.

B GRAMMAR

5 page 65

The Palo Alto Shyness Clinic was founded by Philip Zimbardo, who is a professor at Stanford University, in Palo Alto, California. The clinic provides group and individual therapy for people who are trying to overcome loneliness and shyness. The clinic, which is currently directed by psychologist Dr. Lynn Henderson, uses a specialized treatment model called the Social Fitness Model that trains people in social skills in much the same way that people get trained in physical fitness. Dr. Henderson, who invented the Social Fitness Model, believes that problems of shyness, most of which can be overcome, must be explored in a supportive, positive environment.

D SPEAKING TOPICS

1 page 68

Left Of Center

If you want me
You can find me
Left of center
Off of the strip

In the outskirts
In the fringes
In the corner
Out of the grip

When they ask me
"What are you looking at?"
I always answer
"Nothing much" (not much)
I think they know that
I'm looking at them
I think they think
I must be out of touch

But I'm only
In the outskirts
And in the fringes
On the edge
And off the avenue
And if you want me
You can find me
Left of center
Wondering about you

I think that somehow
Somewhere inside of us
We must be similar
If not the same
So I continue
To be wanting you
Left of center
Against the grain

2 page 70

1. b
2. a
3. c
4. a
5. c

UNIT 4

VOCABULARY FOR COMPREHENSION
2 page 78

1. d	5. k	9. h	13. a
2. i	6. b	10. m	
3. c	7. e	11. g	
4. j	8. f	12. l	

LISTENING FOR MAIN IDEAS, page 79
1. Connectors are people who know a lot of people, are extraordinarily social, and can spread ideas to a lot of people they know.
2. Mavens are people who have specialized knowledge. They are experts in a particular field.
3. Salesmen are people who are incredibly persuasive.

LISTENING FOR DETAILS, page 79
1. False (They are transmitted by a small number of exceptional people.)
2. True
3. False (Only a few recognize between 120 and 130 names.)
4. True
5. True
6. True
7. False (She is not a professional critic. She is just a maven.)
8. False (Many are filled with friends of Ariel's, but not Gladwell's.)
9. True
10. True
11. True
12. True

REACTING TO THE LISTENING
1 page 80

Excerpt One
1. His style is abrupt and businesslike. He orders Gladwell to repeat what he said using the imperative form.

Excerpt Two
2. Although he uses the word *afraid*, he is not fearful. His bold tone of voice and the fact that he interrupted Gladwell to tell the audience he is a connector proves that he is actually a bit boastful of the fact. He uses the word *afraid* to make himself appear modest. Gladwell laughs because he is not really interested and wants to move on.

Excerpt Three
3. He sounds disappointed. He uses the words *epidemic* and he says "restaurants come and go" and his voice indicates a slight feeling of regret.
4. He is impressed by his friend Ariel's power. He re-uses her name to label people like her ("a group of Ariels") and repeats that there are very few people like her.

Excerpt Four
5. Again, he sounds a bit disappointed. He says "Leaves me out. I connect but I can't sell." Gladwell is not really interested in Lydon's point. He coldly repeats what Lydon says and then quickly moves on to explaining salesmen.

2 page 80
1. *Answers will vary.*
2. *Answers will vary.*
3. Some examples of trends are: antibacterial products, flu shots, herbal treatments, the Internet and other technology scams, very high heels, baggy clothes, sport utility vehicles, very small cars, hybrid cars, wind-generated power.

LISTENING TWO
1 page 81

1. b	6. c
2. c	7. c
3. a	8. b
4. c	9. c
5. b	

3 FOCUS ON VOCABULARY
1 page 84

Metaphors Related to Illness
viral marketing / a social epidemic / be immune to an idea / contagious idea / infected / Band-Aid solution

Metaphors Related to Water or Weather
make a splash / float an idea / swim against the tide / a flood of ideas / wave / a ripple effect / the tide is turning

2 page 85
Answers will vary.

3 page 87

1. spreads	9. sneezers
2. contagious	10. ripple effect
3. transmit	11. trigger
4. viral marketing	12. infected
5. come around	13. went through the roof
6. get a hold of	14. ideavirus
7. epidemic	15. went a long way
8. immune	

A PRONUNCIATION

1 page 89

1. sensitívity   criminálity   responsibílity
   populárity
2. energétic   fantástic   realístic
   apologétic
3. transmíssion   organizátion   decísion
   documentátion
4. fináncial   artifícial   commércial
   influéntial
5. lógical   músical   crítical
   theorétical

2 page 89

1. a. áble   b. póssible   c. públic
2. a. invíte   b. inóculate   c. cómplicate
3. a. président   b. bénefit   c. óffice
4. a. cátegory   b. cháos   c. sýmbol

3 page 90

1. a. abílity   3. a. presidéntial
   b. possibílity   b. benefícial
   c. publícity   c. offícial

2. a. invitátion   4. a. categórical
   b. inoculátion   b. chaótic
   c. complicátion   c. symbólic

B GRAMMAR

2 page 92

1. so   9. So
2. that   10. that
3. such   11. such
4. that   12. that
5. so   13. such
6. that   14. that
7. so   15. so
8. that   16. that

3 page 93

1. such popular shoes that
2. so few . . . that
3. such a powerful tool that
4. so anonymous that
5. such an influential theory that
6. so contagious that
7. such a failure that
8. so strongly . . . that

UNIT 5

PREPARING TO LISTEN

2 page 102
Suggested answers:

Clutter: Unfavorable Feng Shui.   **Reason:** Distracting; blocks creativity.

An aquarium: Favorable Feng Shui.   **Reason:** Water symbolizes money.

Plants and flowers: Favorable Feng Shui.   **Reason:** Living things create energy in the room.

The colors red and purple: Favorable Feng Shui.   **Reason:** Associated with light, heat, good luck, and passion; red is a lucky color in China.

Mirrors: Favorable Feng Shui.   **Reason:** Known as the "aspirin" of feng shui, mirrors reflect light and stimulate the ch'i.

A desk facing a view: Unfavorable Feng Shui.   **Reason:** Better to face the door to prevent you from being surprised.

Living near a cemetery: Unfavorable Feng Shui.   **Reason:** Energy in cemetery is sad.

Living on a quiet, dead-end street: Unfavorable Feng Shui.   **Reason:** Negative energy accumulates at the end of the street and there is no place for the ch'i to escape to.

An odd number of dining room chairs: Unfavorable Feng Shui.   **Reason:** Even numbers are lucky; pairs are better.

Pictures of bats on the walls: Favorable Feng Shui.   **Reason:** Bats hang upside down and see the world in a unique way; feng shui encourages creativity and unique thinking.

VOCABULARY FOR COMPREHENSION, page 102

1. b   4. a   7. b   10. a
2. a   5. b   8. a   11. a
3. a   6. a   9. a   12. b

LISTENING FOR MAIN IDEAS, page 105

Part One

2. Feng shui is important in Asia. Lagatree doesn't know if knowledge of feng shui exists in Scandinavia, but clean designs there may reflect feng shui.
3. He uses feng shui to design and build his buildings.
4. Her home office is arranged according to feng shui.

Part Two

5. Mirrors are not desirable in the bedroom, but they are terrific in every other room.
6. She likes it and says it works and, at the very least, it couldn't hurt.
7. Everyone has experienced good feng shui.

LISTENING FOR DETAILS, page 105

Part One

1. It sounds so superstitious.

2. The three examples are: the architecture of buildings, how staircases go up, where buildings are aligned.

3. Norway and Ireland. Her name is Scandinavian because she was named after a Norwegian opera singer, but she identifies as Irish.

4. Having an arrow (the one-way street sign) pointing at your house is unfavorable feng shui.

5. She would have had her back to the door and anyone who came into her office could surprise her. That is bad feng shui.

6. Feng shui has benefited her design. She has a better floor plan than she would have had if she had designed her office herself.

Part Two

7. Mirrors could scare you if you wake up at night or mirrors could also frighten your spirit.

8. They reflect ch'i; they help ch'i circulate; in the dining room or kitchen, mirrors can double your abundance because everything appears twice!

9. She was also skeptical.

10. She would tell them that she didn't believe in feng shui but that they shouldn't tell anyone.

11. Anytime you walk into a room, you get an instinctive feeling about whether you feel good about being there or not.

REACTING TO THE LISTENING

1 page 107

Excerpt One

1. only a superstition

2. silly and ignorant

Excerpt Two

3. feng shui is popular and respected in the United States since Donald Trump is a wealthy and well-known businessman.

4. not a feng shui expert. Thomson is being sarcastic.

Excerpt Three

5. She didn't want anyone to know that perhaps she didn't believe in feng shui entirely, but she was also perhaps a bit embarrassed by her growing interest in it.

B LISTENING TWO, page 108

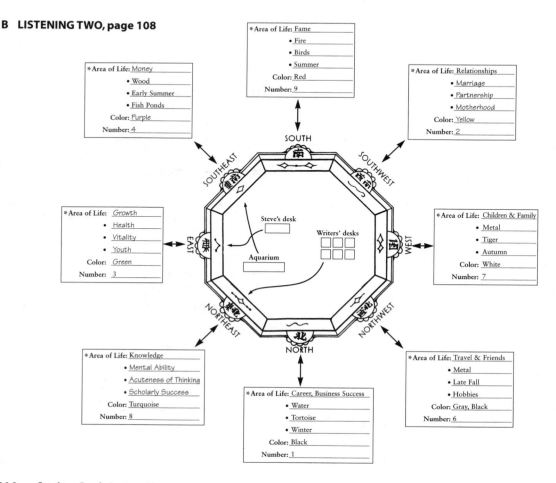

* Area of Life: Fame
  • Fire
  • Birds
  • Summer
  Color: Red
  Number: 9

* Area of Life: Money
  • Wood
  • Early Summer
  • Fish Ponds
  Color: Purple
  Number: 4

* Area of Life: Relationships
  • Marriage
  • Partnership
  • Motherhood
  Color: Yellow
  Number: 2

* Area of Life: Growth
  • Health
  • Vitality
  • Youth
  Color: Green
  Number: 3

* Area of Life: Children & Family
  • Metal
  • Tiger
  • Autumn
  Color: White
  Number: 7

* Area of Life: Knowledge
  • Mental Ability
  • Acuteness of Thinking
  • Scholarly Success
  Color: Turquoise
  Number: 8

* Area of Life: Career, Business Success
  • Water
  • Tortoise
  • Winter
  Color: Black
  Number: 1

* Area of Life: Travel & Friends
  • Metal
  • Late Fall
  • Hobbies
  Color: Gray, Black
  Number: 6

Steve's desk

Writers' desks

Aquarium

SOUTH / SOUTHEAST / SOUTHWEST / EAST / WEST / NORTHEAST / NORTHWEST / NORTH

3 FOCUS ON VOCABULARY

1 page 109

1. got into
2. quote
3. sharp
4. make a move
5. in the midst of
6. aligned
7. talked . . . into
8. work around
9. clean
10. hard-bitten
11. huge
12. rise or fall
13. scared the heck out of
14. keep out
15. peppier
16. can't hurt

A PRONUNCIATION

1 page 112

2. could have lived
3. might have worked
4. wouldn't have died.
5. must have caused
6. could have saved

B GRAMMAR

2 page 114

1. Plus / In addition / On top of that
2. So / As a result
3. But / However
4. In addition / On top of that
5. So / As a result
6. Plus / In addition / On top of that
7. So / As a result

UNIT 6

VOCABULARY FOR COMPREHENSION, page 125

a. 2	e. 16	i. 6	m. 8
b. 5	f. 13	j. 15	n. 4
c. 7	g. 3	k. 11	o. 1
d. 12	h. 14	l. 10	p. 9

LISTENING FOR MAIN IDEAS, page 126

1. c
2. e
3. b
4. d
5. a

LISTENING FOR DETAILS, page 126

1. the prophets of the Old Testament
2. a break from our attachment to material things
3. Although fasting can be stressful, being able to endure a fast can make you stronger spirtually.
4. the first Sunday of every month
5. They give it to poor people.
6. from sunrise to sunset during the month of Ramadan
7. for spiritual well-being
8. Most people don't have time to withdraw from their hectic lives.

REACTING TO THE LISTENING

1 page 127

Excerpt Two

Patterson's words: discipline, working, making decisions, forming the will
My own words: *Answers will vary.*

Excerpt Three

Ahmed's words: withdraw during the day, replenishment of the soul, spirtually exhausted
My own words: *Answers will vary.*

B LISTENING TWO, page 128

1. a, c   2. c, d, e   3. b, d   4. a, b   5. a, b, e, f

3 FOCUS ON VOCABULARY

1 page 131

a. 14	e. 4	i. 13	l. 6
b. 12	f. 2	j. 9	m. 11
c. 3	g. 5	k. 10	n. 8
d. 7	h. 1		

A PRONUNCIATION

2 page 133

1. 3	4. —	7. —	10. —
2. —	5. 1	8. 3	11. 2
3. 1	6. 2	9. 1	12. —

B GRAMMAR

2 page 135

1. NC
2. C / NC
3. C / NC
4. C / NC
5. C
6. NC
7. NC
8. NC
9. C
10. C
11. C
12. C
13. C
14. C / NC
15. NC
16. C / NC
17. C / NC
18. C / NC

3 page 136

2. a. NC / a great deal of
   b. C / X
3. a. NC / a lot of
   b. C / fewer
4. a. C / a great many
   b. NC / very little
5. a. NC / quite a bit of
   b. C / a large number of
6. a. C / certain / many
   b. NC / a great deal of
7. a. NC / X (the)
   b. C / X (their)

1. a little
2. little
3. a little
4. few
5. little
6. a few
7. little
8. little
9. a few
10. Few
11. little
12. few
13. a little

UNIT 7

VOCABULARY FOR COMPREHENSION, page 149

a. 8
b. 13
c. 6
d. 1
e. 10
f. 14
g. 7
h. 4
i. 15
j. 9
k. 11
l. 5
m. 2
n. 12
o. 3

LISTENING FOR MAIN IDEAS, page 150

Part One

1. It is very common.
2. He warns that any employee may be under surveillance at any time.
3. They have the right to know how equipment is being used, if rules are being obeyed, and if employees are getting the job done.

Part Two

4. Monitoring can deter theft and also protect workers.
5. Surveillance practices demean workers.
6. Employees should be informed when monitored and there should be no monitoring in private places.

Part Three

7. It prohibits eavesdropping on private phone calls.
8. It can raise levels of worker stress and lead to lower productivity.

LISTENING FOR DETAILS, page 151

Part One

2. F (nearly two-thirds)
3. T
4. F (by 100%)
5. F (He does not believe it is morally wrong.)
6. F (The U.S. Postal Service monitors the length of time to deliver the mail.)

Part Two

7. F (They keep a log so that employees can pay for personal calls.)
8. F (They monitor e-mail to protect employees from sexual harassment and racial slurs.)
9. T
10. F (She concedes there are some legitimate reasons.)
11. F (They should always be told.)

Part Three

12. F (Most states allow surveillance in private places.)
13. T
14. F (Employers do have the right to monitor the length of personal phone calls.)
15. T
16. T

REACTING TO THE LISTENING

1 page 153

Excerpt Two

3.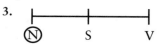

4. He uses the phrase "Big Brother is watching and whatever." He also says . . . "that's a cheap shot."

Excerpt Three

5.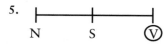

6. She uses "certainly" and "do not need." Her tone is firm and decisive.

Excerpt Four

7.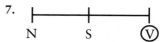

8. She uses "whatsoever." Her tone is commanding and resolute.

3 FOCUS ON VOCABULARY

1 page 156

1. going that extra mile
2. concede
3. fine line
4. scope
5. thought twice about
6. was all well and good
7. stepped up
8. kept tabs
9. cheap shot
10. subject to
11. morale
12. leave . . . at the door
13. legitimate

A PRONUNCIATION

2 page 159

1. The ACLU director was shocked by the íncrease (N) in monitoring and was afraid that willy-nilly surveillance would continue to increáse. (V)
2. We decided to condúct (V) a comprehensive survey to measure employee cónduct. (N)
3. The óbject (N) of my presentation is simply to objéct (V) to the use of secret surveillance.
4. The boss suspécts (V) that she is the only súspect (N) in the case involving the stolen computer files.
5. She got a special pérmit (N) that would permít (V) her to see confidential employee information.
6. We all had to keep a special récord (N) in order to recórd (V) all personal phone calls.
7. Why do you have to insúlt (V) me with all those ínsults? (N) Just tell me how to fix the mistakes.
8. We're pleased with your prógress (N) in your job so far, but you'll have to progréss (V) even further before getting promoted.
9. As hard as I tried to settle the cónflict (N) with my boss, our opinions continued to conflíct (V) over certain key issues.
10. The company projécts (V) big profits from these prójects. (N)

B GRAMMAR

2 page 161

1. a
   b
2. b
   a
3. a
   b
4. b
   a

5. b
   a
6. a
   b
7. b
   a

3 page 163

1. matching / to match
2. hiring
3. reading
4. testing
5. interviewing
6. to provide
7. to ask
8. to question
9. to make
10. administering
11. using
12. asking
13. taking
14. revealing

UNIT 8

VOCABULARY FOR COMPREHENSION, page 172

a. 3
b. 14
c. 8
d. 5
e. 12
f. 13
g. 1
h. 11
i. 10
j. 2
k. 4
l. 6
m. 9
n. 7

LISTENING FOR MAIN IDEAS, page 174

Part One

2. ICRC's position of neutrality
3. international human rights and the laws of war

Part Two

4. ratified by hundreds of countries; basic rules of war
5. U.S. subscribed to Geneva Conventions
6. not white, Western European values; human universals

Part Three

7. one of the oldest moral traditions, warrior's honor and responsibility to protect community
8. task is dangerous, men must learn to restrain aggression and use war for benefit of community
9. war is so devastating; now equated with barbarism; morality cannot prevail
10. every culture contains elements of warrior's honor, which should restrain people

LISTENING FOR DETAILS, page 175

Part One	Part Two	Part Three
1. a	6. b	11. a
2. a	7. a	12. c
3. c	8. b	13. b
4. c	9. b	14. c
5. b	10. b	

REACTING TO THE LISTENING

1 page 176

Excerpt One

1. This is the tradition set forth by the U.N. in 1948 when it adopted the Universal Declaration of Human Rights, which said, "All human beings are born free and equal in dignity and rights . . ." The modern human rights tradition sees war as a moral violation and feels human rights activists cannot remain neutral.
2. They are familiar with the U.N. and other well-known human rights organizations like Amnesty International.

Excerpt Two

3. protect civilians; do not torture prisoners; do not shoot noncombatants
4. human suffering should be limited; war victims should be protected

Excerpt Three

5. He has a positive and respectful attitude toward the position of the ICRC. He says that the warrior's honor is one of the "oldest moral traditions," and he stresses the word *simply* to imply that the ICRC merely wants to institutionalize what is already a very old and enduring tradition.

6. Soldiers behaving according to the rules of war will behave with honor and lessen the human suffering incurred by war.

B LISTENING TWO, page 177

Part One

1. T
2. F
3. T

Part Two

4. T
5. F
6. T

Part Three

7. F
8. T
9. F
10. T

Part Four

11. F
12. F
13. T

3 FOCUS ON VOCABULARY

2 page 179

1. b a	2. b c a	3. a b
4. b a c	5. b a	6. a b
7. b a	8. b c a	9. a b c
10. b a		

4 page 183

a. 9	g. 10	l. 15
b. 5	h. 2	m. 11
c. 12	i. 4	n. 7
d. 14	j. 8	o. 6
e. 3	k. 16	p. 13
f. 1		

A PRONUNCIATION

3 page 185

1. cot
2. cap
3. luck
4. nut
5. hot
6. lag

5 page 186

CUP–CUP (column 1):

government funding / a bloody struggle / love of country

CAP–CAP (column 2):

natural disasters / savage attack / a challenging task

CUP–COP (column 3):

public controversy / gun shots / a tough job / combatant's conduct

CUP–CAP (column 4):

cultural values / floods and famines / a bloody battle

CAP–CUP (column 5):

lack of money / a practical discovery

UNIT 9

VOCABULARY FOR COMPREHENSION

2 page 197

1. i	7. b
2. a	8. k
3. d	9. c
4. f	10. h
5. l	11. g
6. e	12. j

LISTENING FOR MAIN IDEAS, page 198

Part One

1. b
2. c
3. a
4. c

Part Two

5. c
6. b
7. a

LISTENING FOR DETAILS, page 200

Part One

Researcher's Name: Martin Gardiner

Experiment Location: Rhode Island

Research Subjects: 6- and 7-year-olds

Purpose of Study: impact of arts training on reading and math

Frequency of Classes, Control Group: Standard curriculum

music: 2 ×/month

art: 2 ×/month

Frequency of Classes, Experimental Group:

Special arts classes: 2 ×/week

Style of Instruction, Control Group: music lessons were passive

Style of Instruction, Experimental Group: arts program was active

Skills Taught: Art and Music, Control Group: listened to concerts, talked about music

Skills Taught: Art and Music, Experimental Group: sang together, drew shapes

Results: 1. Kids who started below average caught up to average in reading. 2. Kids were ahead in math. 3. Kids continued to improve in math.

Part Two

Researcher's Name: Frances Rauscher

Experiment Location: University of Wisconsin

Research Subjects: 3-years-old

Purpose of Study: impact of arts education on math ability

Skills Taught: Art and Music, Experimental group: piano and singing lessons

Results: 1. Children scored higher in IQ test of abstract reasoning. 2. Children understand proportions and ratios.

B LISTENING TWO, page 202

Part Two

The Relationship between Music and Math

- both involved with filling puzzles
- math is used to set out beats to music
- music is highly mathematical
- patterns of neural cell firing (stimulation) are similar
- both involve same part of the brain

So, in short, one of the reasons that math and music are so similar is that the same part of the brain is used for both functions.

Part Three

Warren's and Sharon's Reactions to the Research

- scared
- excited by significant role
- fear that opportunities may have been missed

In other words, Sharon and Warren feel that it's important for parents to play an active role in their children's development in order to tap their children's full abilities.

Part Four

Things to Do with Your Child

- do simple things
- pay attention to child
- play kind of games grandmother used to play

In other words, Sharon suggests that you simply give your child a lot of attention.

3 FOCUS ON VOCABULARY

1 **page 203**

2.	a.	F	applause
	b.	L	large-sized hands
3.	a.	L	arranged the music (of)
	b.	F	strategically planned
4.	a.	L	thin, thread-like metal to conduct electricity
	b.	F	neural (brain) connections
5.	a.	L	glass or screen openings in a wall that let in light and air
	b.	F	opportunities for learning and stimulation
6.	a.	F	failed
	b.	L	stopped the electricity
7	a.	F	get angry
	b.	L	explode
8	a.	L	physically marked (on the skin)
	b.	F	emotionally or psychologically hurt or damaged

3 **page 207**

1. e	3. c	5. h	7. g	9. b
2. d	4. f	6. i	8. a	

A PRONUNCIATION

2 **page 210**

1. typical lesson
2. self-esteem
3. research challenge
4. standard curriculum
5. art classes
6. critical ingredients
7. boost brain power
8. an interactive approach
9. logical thinking

B GRAMMAR

2 page 212

1. are being researched
2. is being studied
3. appeared
4. can be enhanced
5. can be improved
6. were involved
7. were divided
8. received
9. was provided
10. were given
11. had been given
    (were given)
12. consisted
13. had . . . collected
14. had . . . analyzed
15. emerged
16. had been instruced
    (were instructed)
17. concluded
18. had been used
    (was used)
19. scored
20. seemed
21. may be simulated
22. are strengthened
23. appear
24. are fired
25. are performed
26. had . . . repeated

3 page 214

Student A

2. was . . . sparked
3. was . . . pushed
5. was told; had . . .
   made; was sent
6. has . . . been done
7. have been chosen
8. will be selected;
   will be printed

Student B

2. might have been
   inspired; was given
3. was encouraged;
   pushed; was identified
4. should have been
   noticed
5. was asked
6. are handled;
   have . . . repaired;
   get . . . dry-cleaned;
   have . . . taken;
   must be done
7. is being considered;
   is chosen;
   have been invited

UNIT 10

BACKGROUND, page 221
Suggested answers:

1. TI
2. USG, P
3. USG
4. TI, FSS
5. TI
6. TI
7. USG
8. P
9. TI, FSS, P
10. TI, FSS

VOCABULARY FOR COMPREHENSION, page 222

1. a
2. b
3. b
4. a
5. a
6. a
7. b
8. a
9. a
10. a

LISTENING FOR MAIN IDEAS, page 224

Part One

1. It is necessary to program the V-chip device to automatically block sex and violence from TV.
2. the government and the public
3. probably not

Part Two

4. prime-time shows and movies
5. the whole show

Part Three

6. It'll take time for the V-chip to be accepted throughout the culture. It'll take time for people to buy new TV sets with V-chips. Television shows that are forbidden will interest young people.
7. It was successful.

LISTENING FOR DETAILS, page 225

Part One

1. T
2. F (He wants the industry to develop the system.)
3. T
4. F (It's not a panacea, but it will help.)

Part Two

5. T
6. T
7. F (The V-chip doesn't block out shows permanently. Parents can lock it and unlock it.)

Part Three

8. F (Parents will need to buy new TV sets.)
9. T
10. F (Canadians experimented with 250 families.)
11. F (It was very successful even though it was a very elaborate system.)
12. F (Canadians love violence less than Americans.)

REACTING TO THE LISTENING

1 page 226

Excerpt One

1. poor
2. He says they are "trashy" and emphasizes that they lack news *and* entertainment with the structure "neither . . . nor . . ."
3. He laughs to imply he agrees with Marin.

Excerpt Two

4. a show for adults or mature audiences
5. not "wholesome"; he contrasts *NYPD Blue* with more wholesome shows using the construct "when . . . then when"

Excerpt Three

6. Yes, he does. He uses a matter-of-fact, casual tone of voice to imply that it is well known or obvious. He says, "studies have shown," "any of us who were kids remember," "there was one study."
7. He agrees with a laugh.

B LISTENING TWO, page 227

Checks on 1, 3, 6, 7

3 FOCUS ON VOCABULARY

1 page 228

1. b	6. d
2. e	7. c
3. f	8. j
4. a	9. h
5. g	10. i

2 page 229

1. media	7. forbidden fruit
2. trashy	8. invariably
3. wholesome	9. bread-and-butter
4. notion	10. hypocritical
5. take	11. swallow
6. panacea	12. falls under

A PRONUNCIATION

1 page 232

2. So you could presumably program your TV to <u>pick úp</u> shows that were either G or PG rated.
3. . . . but if you <u>stick wíth</u> your old set for another ten years . . .
4. All the families that <u>tried</u> it <u>óut</u>, loved it.
5. We <u>caught úp with</u> him in Sydney, Australia.
6. You should be flattered that TV is <u>taking úp</u> your model.
7. Rick Marin, a magazine editor, <u>looked ínto</u> the debate over TV ratings.
8. Manufacturers are reluctantly <u>putting</u> them <u>ín</u>.

B GRAMMAR

2 page 235

1. It could / may / might help . . .
2. Yes, they should / ought to be able to understand it.
3. They think he may / might / could have copied a crime he saw on TV.
4. It couldn't (possibly) have happened.
5. Hmm . . . it must have been blocked out.
6. Yes, it should have gotten an MA rating . . .
7. They couldn't (possibly) rate all of them.
8. Yes, some could / may / might make the effort, but most parents won't bother.

Unit Word List

The **Unit Word List** is a summary of key vocabulary from the Student Book's Vocabulary for Comprehension and Focus on Vocabulary sections. The words are presented by unit, in alphabetical order.

Unit 1

addiction
anxious
be bombarded with
be going on
chat room
come out
compulsiveness
depressed
devote
driven
engage in
enhance
enhancement
feed (verb)
feel empty
fulfillment
go through

high-tech
isolate
multitask (verb)
noodle around
overwhelmed
present with
problematic
put together
shape (verb)
social interactions
strategize
support group
surf (verb)
symptom
therapy
turn into
turn someone in

Unit 2

access
assess
boardroom
burn out
callous
civic
dictate
Disneyphiles
engineer (verb)
envision
evolve
hotter than hell
idealistic
landscape
laudable

live by
make ends meet
nostalgia
nurture
play out
scrutiny
self-selecting
small-town America
spirituality
sprawling
thwart
town planning
unscripted
vibrant

Unit 3

adverse
aloof
assertive
bashful
bold
break the ice
chronic
condescending
draw out
extroverted
fill the void
gloomy
gregarious
handicap
in the first place
inhibited
introvert
killjoy
kindred souls
life of the party
mark (verb)
merit
misattributions
negative
open
optimist

outgoing
outlook
pessimist
petrified
phobia
Pollyanna
positive
reserved
reticent
self-conscious
shrinking violet
sociable
social butterfly
standoffish
syndrome
take things as they come
talk a blue streak
think of oneself as
timid
upbeat
virtually
wallflower
whiny
widespread
wind up

Unit 4

a flood of ideas
a ripple effect
a social epidemic
Band-aid solution
be consumed by
be immune to an idea
be triggered by
come around
contagious
contagious idea
crime wave
epidemic
float an idea
flood (verb)
generate
get a hold of
go a long way toward
go through the roof
hold (verb)
ideavirus

immune
infect
infected
make a splash
maven
profile (verb)
relentless
root (noun)
sneezers
spread (verb)
swim against the tide
the tide turns
transmission
transmit
trigger (noun)
viral marketing
wave (noun)
win someone over
word-of-mouth

Unit 5

abundance
align
anecdotes
be caught off guard
can't hurt to
circulate
clean (adjective)
frown upon
get into
hard-bitten
huge
in the midst of
keep out

make a move
make digressions
peppy
quote (verb)
rise or fall
scare the heck out of
sense (verb)
sharp
skeptically
talk someone into
transcendent
work around

Unit 6

ascetic
catch on
discipline (noun)
divine
draw a person out
enact
fast (verb)
foster
gratitude
hectic
humility
notion
over time

pervasive
prophet
pull back
quest (noun)
refrain from
replenish
royalties
take on
trace back
vibrant
well-being
will (noun)

Unit 7

be all well and good
be subject to
Big Brother
cheap shot
concede
demeaned
deter
dignity
drive (verb)
eavesdrop on
fine line
go that extra mile
keep an eye on

keep tabs on
leave . . . at the door
legitimate
log (noun)
morale
racial slurs
safeguard
scope (noun)
sinister
step up
surveillance
think twice about
willy-nilly

Unit 8

accept
access (noun)
advice
advise
affect (verb)
alternative ethic
assure
barbarism
code
council
counsel (verb and noun)
counterintuitive
devastating
disinterested
disseminate
do without
draft evader
drawn to
effect (verb and noun)
eminent
ensure
equate
except

excess
get at
house-and-garden
human universal
identify
imminent
imply
infer
institutionalize
legitimacy
live by
prevail
principal
principle
ratify
restrain
savagery
spare
subscribe
tame (verb)
uninterested
unleash
volatile

Unit 9

a big hand
abstract reasoning
advance (verb)
as a whole
attack (verb)
blow it
blow up
blow up at
boost
building blocks
catch up to
curriculum
do more for
dramatically
enhance

hallmark
have nothing to do with
intervention
neurological
orchestrate
proficiency
regardless of
scarred
self-esteem
sequential
underscore
well-rounded
window
wiring (noun)
work in progress

Unit 10

bread-and-butter
counteract
disgust (verb)
fall under (a category)
forbidden fruit
hypocritical
invariably
media
notion
offensive
panacea

pledge (verb)
prime-time
put the fox in charge of
    the henhouse
swallow (verb)
take
tidal wave
trashy
voluntary
wholesome

Introduction to Achievement Tests

The following reproducible Achievement Tests allow teachers to evaluate students' progress and to identify any areas where the students might have problems in developing their listening and speaking skills. The Achievement Tests should be given upon completion of the corresponding Student Book unit.

Description   There are two Achievement Tests for each unit. **Test 1** is a "paper and pencil" test of receptive skills. It assesses students' mastery of listening comprehension and of the vocabulary, pronunciation, and grammar points introduced in the unit.

Test 2 is intended to assess the students' productive, or speaking, skills. It consists of a speaking task related to the content of the unit. Each speaking task is designed to elicit a speech sample lasting several minutes.

Administration   Administration of **Test 1** requires use of the recorded material on the audio CD packaged with this Teacher's Manual. Students will need to listen to the audio program in order to answer the questions in each section of the test. The answer key to the tests and the audioscript of the material on the CD are included at the end of the Achievement Test section.

Teachers can decide how to incorporate **Test 2** (the speaking task) into their testing situations. Some teachers will assign each speaking task immediately after students complete **Test 1**; others may decide to set aside another time to complete it. The tasks may be set up for pairs, small groups, the whole class, or on a teacher-to-student basis. When set up for pairs or small groups, teachers will need to circulate around the classroom and spend enough time with each pair or group to evaluate the production of individual students.

Some teachers may not find it possible to evaluate all of the students on every speaking test. As an alternative, teachers may choose to evaluate only part of a class on a given **Test 2** speaking task and evaluate the remaining students on tests given at a later time. Teachers may also choose to evaluate students only on every other test or on a total of three or four tests over the term.

Scoring Test 1   Individual test items are worth one point, for a maximum total of 30 points per test. To facilitate scoring, an answer key is provided at the end of the book. A student's score can be obtained by adding together the number of correct items. To obtain an overall "listening score" for a student, teachers may average all of the **Test 1** scores that the student received in the class.

Scoring Test 2   Speaking tasks are evaluated holistically using the categories in the rating sheet that follows. The categories include content, vocabulary, pronunciation, and grammar. In each category, 0 indicates poor or inadequate performance for the level; 1 indicates average or acceptable performance; 2 indicates good or outstanding performance. The teacher circles the rating for each category and adds the numbers to obtain a total score out of 8 possible points.

Test 2 Rating Sheet

Student: _____   Unit _____

Content	0	1	2
Vocabulary	0	1	2
Pronunciation	0	1	2
Grammar	0	1	2

Total Score _____

The teacher can complete the rating sheet for each student's test and give it to the student. It can also be kept by the teacher as a record of each student's progress.

An overall "speaking score" for a student may be obtained by averaging all of the **Test 2** scores the student received in the class.

Achievement Tests
Unit 1

Name: _____

Date: _____

TEST 1

A. ☐ **1** *Listen to the excerpt. Mark the sentences **T** (true) or **F** (false).*

_____ 1. The interviewer wants to know if multitasking increases people's intelligence.

_____ 2. The speaker believes that people are getting smarter in every way.

_____ 3. A mixture of unrelated ideas can enhance creativity.

_____ 4. The speaker thinks that multitasking is a threat to people's creativity.

☐ **2** *Listen to the excerpt again. Circle the answer that best completes each sentence.*

1. Research reports a recent increase in IQ of up to _____.
   a. 30 points
   b. 20 points
   c. 80 points

2. Multitasking can enhance a person's ability to _____.
   a. read a book
   b. complete an SAT test
   c. noodle around with others about ideas

3. Creativity _____.
   a. is enhanced by answering every e-mail
   b. requires fast decisions
   c. happens slowly

4. A creative person probably would not _____.
   a. be concerned about answering every e-mail
   b. enjoy a mixture of unrelated ideas
   c. read a book about history or a philosopher

B. *Listen to each sentence. In the blank, write the letter of the definition or synonym that best completes the sentence.*

_____ 1.

_____ 2.

_____ 3.

_____ 4.

_____ 5.

a. treatment of problems by talking about them

b. looking for information

c. people who meet to help each other with a problem they all share

d. show an illness by having a particular type of behavior or condition

e. unable to control certain behavior

C. *Listen to each statement. Circle the letter of the sentence with a similar meaning.*

1. **a.** They are becoming addicted to their jobs.
   b. They are becoming interested in their jobs.

2. **a.** They don't care about what's going on at work.
   b. They don't want to feel left out of the action.

3. **a.** They seem to think that their personal lives aren't important.
   b. They value their personal time.

4. **a.** They like to play with ideas.
   b. They want to keep up with their e-mail.

5. **a.** They have to do many jobs.
   b. They do one job very well.

6. **a.** They do one task at a time.
   b. They feel attacked by all the different tasks.

7. **a.** They feel that they can do their jobs well.
   b. They feel that there is too much to do.

D. *Listen to the sentences. Circle the word that is highlighted in each sentence.*

1. My roommate spends hours on the Internet every day.

2. When does he do his homework?

3. That's the problem—he doesn't.

4. Then he's not going to pass his classes.

5. I know, but all he cares about is his computer.

E. *Listen to the first part of each exchange. Complete each exchange with an appropriate short-answer wish statement.*

1. Yes, and I wish he _____.

2. No, but I wish he _____.

3. No, but I wish I _____.

4. Yes, but I almost wish I _____.

5. I don't think so, but I wish you _____.

TEST 2

Make a list of things that you wish you could do. For example, you might want to start by saying, "I wish I could climb Mount Everest."

When you have made your list, talk about two or three of the things that you wish you could do. Talk to your partner, small group, or class about what the conditions would need to be for your wish to come true. Use wish statements and conditional statements.

Achievement Tests
Unit 2

Name: _____

Date: _____

TEST 1

A. **1** *Listen to the excerpt. Mark the sentences T (true) or F (false).*

_____ 1. The planners of Celebration tried to make it like a town from the 1940s.

_____ 2. Porches were built on houses to encourage interaction among neighbors.

_____ 3. People in Celebration enjoyed sitting outside on their porches.

2 *Listen to the excerpt again. Read the questions and circle the best answer.*

1. According to the interviewer, what was true about some of the designs from the 1940s?
   a. They didn't work very well in the 1990s.
   b. They were very useful in designing the new town.
   c. They existed only in people's imaginations.

2. According to the speaker, what did the planners envision when they designed the houses with porches?
   a. People would be nostalgic for the 1940s.
   b. People would ride their bikes on the streets.
   c. People would be outside talking with their neighbors.

3. What does the speaker say about central Florida?
   a. It is uncomfortably hot much of the year.
   b. There are many people walking down the streets and riding their bikes.
   c. The porches have air conditioning.

B. *Listen to each sentence. Circle the letter of the sentence below that is most similar in meaning to the sentence you hear.*

1. **a.** It is exciting and energetic at night.
   b. It is quiet and peaceful at night.

2. **a.** Outsiders do not pay much attention to utopian societies.
   b. Outsiders give utopian societies a thorough and detailed examination.

3. **a.** They try to help community ties develop and grow.
   b. They try to imagine community ties.

4. **a.** They feel slightly sad when they remember past happy events.
   b. They are glad that the past is over.

5. **a.** It is insensitive and uncaring.
   b. It is admirable.

6. **a.** The community should include the ability to enter undeveloped areas.
   b. The community should spread over a wide area.

7. **a.** The community was evaluated by the media.
   b. The media imagined what the community would be like.

8. **a.** They thought that it was very admirable.
   b. They thought that it was insensitive and unkind.

 C. *Listen to each sentence. In the blank, write the letter of the definition or synonym that best completes the sentence.*

_____ 1.   **a.** follow or obey

_____ 2.   **b.** end up

_____ 3.   **c.** have enough money to live on

_____ 4.   **d.** exhausted, extremely tired

 D. *Listen to the sentences. Each sentence contains **as, has, is,** or **–es,** pronounced /əz/. Circle the one you hear in each sentence.*

1. **a.** as   **b.** has   **c.** is   **d.** –es

2. **a.** as   **b.** has   **c.** is   **d.** –es

3. **a.** as   **b.** has   **c.** is   **d.** –es

4. **a.** as   **b.** has   **c.** is   **d.** –es

5. **a.** as   **b.** has   **c.** is   **d.** –es

🎧 **E.** *Imagine that you are being interviewed about your utopian community. Listen to each question. Write an answer using the cues provided. Add words where necessary.*

1. preferable / a person / check / my Website

   _____

2. insist / all houses / paint / white

   _____

3. recommend / roofs / be / red tile

   _____

4. vital / each resident / submit / plans / first

   _____

5. essential / lawns / look / the same

   _____

6. propose / residents / plant / cactus

   _____

7. suggest / that person / not move / to my utopia

   _____

TEST 2

You are thinking about moving into a new community that is being built. The developer has asked you for advice about what to include in the new community.

Tell your partner, small group, or class the advice you would give the developer. Use verbs of urgency such as ***demand*** and ***insist.*** For example, you might want to say, "I insist that my house have a porch."

Achievement Tests
Unit 3

Name: _____

Date: _____

TEST 1

A. ☐1 *Listen to the excerpt. Mark the sentences **T** (true) or **F** (false).*

_____ 1. Julie Danis' co-worker is grouchy.

_____ 2. Julie wants to be optimistic like her co-worker.

☐2 *Listen to the excerpt again. Circle the answer that best completes each sentence.*

1. Julie is annoyed by her co-worker's
   a. grouchy mood.   **b.** blurred vision.   **c.** "find the bright side" philosophy.

2. Julie believes that an optimistic outlook
   a. has some merits.   **b.** has no merit.   **c.** is impossible.

3. According to Julie, when someone says, "You can't cry over something that can't cry over you," you should
   a. throw lemons at them.   **b.** say, "Yes I can."   **c.** make lemonade.

B. *Listen to the sentences. Complete the restatement of each sentence below with the appropriate definition or synonym from the list.*

adverse	kindred souls	aloof	merit
condescending	a phobia	an extrovert	reticent

1. These people seem _____, but they are really just very shy.

2. Shy people don't want to keep themselves _____.

3. Mary could not have fun at parties because she was not _____.

4. Mary became very _____ in a large group.

5. Her shyness began to have an _____ effect.

6. Her fear became so serious that it was _____.

7. The therapist helped Mary realize that her thoughts had

   _____.

8. Mary and her best friend are _____.

C. *Listen to each sentence. In the blank, write the letter of the definition or synonym that best completes the sentence.*

_____ 1.	**a.** break the ice
_____ 2.	**b.** fill the void
_____ 3.	**c.** mark
_____ 4.	**d.** think of
_____ 5.	**e.** wind up
_____ 6.	**f.** in the first place
_____ 7.	**g.** outlook
_____ 8.	**h.** draw out

 D. *Listen to each sentence. Circle the letter of the one you hear.*

1. **a.** Her co-worker said, "She's got a project to finish."
   b. Her co-worker said she's got a project to finish.

2. **a.** My co-worker says Julie makes lemonade out of lemons.
   b. "My co-worker," says Julie, "makes lemonade out of lemons."

3. **a.** You need to see the therapist who is an expert on shyness.
   b. You need to see the therapist, who is an expert on shyness.

E. *Listen to each pair of sentences. The second sentence of each pair is in the list. Use the list to make adjective clauses and complete the sentences. Add commas where necessary.*

> She had a problem with chronic shyness.
> This woman's interests were the same as hers.
> She met other shy people there.
> She found the meetings very helpful.
> Both of these helped her.
> She would feel more confident at that time.

1. Mary _____ began to attend

   support group meetings.

2. Mary met another woman _____.

3. Mary enjoyed attending the support group meetings _____

   _____.

4. Mary never missed her meetings _____.

5. Mary continued to attend the meetings and meet with her therapist _____

   _____.

6. Mary looked forward to a time _____.

TEST 2

You have just arrived at a party where you do not know people. You are going to introduce yourself and talk about something shared, for example, the weather or a current news topic.

Tell your partner, small group, or class what you would say. Use appropriate language to introduce yourself, break the ice, and maintain the conversation.

Achievement Tests Unit 4

Name: _____

Date: _____

TEST 1

A. **1** *Listen to the excerpt. Mark the sentences **T** (true) or **F** (false).*

_____ 1. In the 1980s, the New York subway system was dangerous.

_____ 2. The subway did not change very dramatically after the cleanup took place.

_____ 3. A clean subway shows that no one is in charge.

2 *Listen to the excerpt again. Circle the answer that best completes each sentence.*

1. The man in charge of cleaning up the subway system _____.
   a. believed in the broken windows theory
   b. arrested all the killers and robbers
   c. was crazy

2. The man who directed cleaning up the subway system got rid of _____.
   a. the broken windows
   b. litter, graffiti, and turnstile jumpers
   c. the cops by the turnstiles

3. Litter, graffiti, and turnstile jumping are examples of _____.
   a. serious crimes
   b. tipping points
   c. assault

B. *Listen to each sentence. In the blank, write the letter of the definition or synonym that best completes the sentence.*

_____ 1.   a. an epidemic

_____ 2.   b. a maven

_____ 3.   c. relentless

_____ 4.   d. generate

_____ 5.   e. won them over

_____ 6.   f. word-of-mouth

_____ 7.   g. the root

C. *Listen to the sentences. Complete the restatement of each sentence below with the appropriate word or expression from the list.*

Band-Aid solution	wave	contagious idea
a ripple effect	made a splash	swimming against the tide
triggered		

1. Rachel Carson's book really _____.

2. She found that DDT use had _____ on the environment.

3. At the time, Rachel Carson was _____ by suggesting that DDT not be used.

4. Her conclusions _____ a government investigation.

5. What the chemical companies wanted was just a _____.

6. Rachel Carson's concern for the environment was a _____.

7. Her ideas were the first _____ of many environmentally conscious decisions that came later.

D. *Listen to the words. Put a stress mark (') over the stressed syllable in each word.*

1. transmission
2. chaotic
3. sensitivity
4. theoretical
5. influential

E. *Listen to the sentences about Rachel Carson's* Silent Spring. *Complete each sentence below with* **so** *or* **such** *and the appropriate word or phrase from the list.*

angry   careful research   afraid   convinced   an important message

1. Magazine publishers were _____ of losing advertisers that they refused to publish Rachel Carson's article.

2. Rachel Carson felt that she had _____ that she decided to write a book.

3. Some people in the chemical industry were _____ that they attacked Rachel Carson personally and questioned her conclusions.

4. Rachel Carson had done _____ that respected experts supported her.

5. The government was _____ of the harmful effects of DDT that the chemical was finally banned.

TEST 2

You want to influence your classmates to purchase a certain product. Bring an everyday product (for example, a pencil) to class.

Describe the good points of your product to your partner, small group, or class. Use appropriate vocabulary from the unit and *so* or *such* to describe your product.

TEST 1

A. ☐1 *Listen to the excerpt. Mark the sentences **T** (true) or **F** (false).*

_____ **1.** According to most people, Bruce Lee should never have purchased his house.

_____ **2.** The feng shui in Bruce Lee's backyard was good because of the valley.

_____ **3.** According to most people, Bruce Lee's death could have been avoided.

☐2 *Listen to the excerpt again. Circle the answer that best completes each sentence.*

1. The ch'i around Bruce Lee's house was affected by _____.
   a. the trees
   b. the wind
   c. Hong Kong

2. In order to change his feng shui, Bruce Lee used _____.
   a. a mirror
   b. kung fu
   c. a storm

3. The tree and the mirror _____.
   a. were replaced immediately after a storm
   b. were destroyed by a storm
   c. destroyed the ch'i in the backyard

B. *Listen to each sentence. In the blank, write the letter of the definition or synonym that best completes the sentence.*

_____ **1.**   **a.** disapprove of something

_____ **2.**   **b.** a personal story

_____ **3.**   **c.** experienced and tough

_____ **4.**   **d.** beyond the limits of ordinary
                           experience
_____ **5.**
                        e. feel and know
_____ **6.**
                        f. with doubt

C. *Listen to the sentences. Complete the restatement of each sentence below with the appropriate expression from the list.*

couldn't hurt	rise or fall
got into	scare the heck out of
in the midst of	talked into
make a move	work around

1. My friend _____ me _____ doing it.

2. I was _____ studying for exams.

3. My friend said my career wouldn't _____ if I took a short break.

4. They _____ me!

5. I decided it _____.

6. I had been afraid to _____.

7. I really _____ it.

8. I have been able to _____ my exam schedule.

D. *Listen to the sentences. Fill in the blanks with the modal perfect forms.*

1. If my friend hadn't convinced me, I _____ my room around.

2. I probably _____ that night, but I wanted to take a break.

3. Without my friend's help, I _____ the changes.

4. My friend _____ this type of thing before.

5. I can't believe how good my room looks! I _____ this a long time ago!

E. *Listen to each pair of sentences. The second sentence contains a discourse connector. In the blank for each sentence, write the correct type of discourse connector from the list.*

　　　　contrast　　　　addition　　　　result

　　　1. _____

　　　2. _____

　　　3. _____

　　　4. _____

　　　5. _____

TEST 2

Think about some contrasting traditions of the East and West, such as chopsticks and forks, or celebrating Buddha's birthday and celebrating Hanukkah.

Talk to your partner, small group, or class about a tradition from the East or West. Describe the different aspects of the tradition. As you talk, be sure to use discourse connectors.

Achievement Tests
Unit 6

Name: _____

Date: _____

TEST 1

A. **1** *Listen to the excerpt. Mark the sentences **T** (true) or **F** (false).*

_____ 1. Wat Tham Krabat was a typical forest monastery.

_____ 2. The monastery's work with outside issues did not affect its daily schedule.

_____ 3. The monastery worked with both children and adults.

2 *Listen to the excerpt again. Circle the answer that best completes each sentence.*

1. Wat Tham Krabat monastery worked with _____.
   a. AIDS patients, Westerners, and refugees
   b. Hmong refugees and Western AIDS patients
   c. AIDS patients, refugees, and drug addicts

2. The refugees were from _____.
   a. Laos
   b. Cambodia
   c. Vietnam

3. Wat Tham Krabat monastery is unusual because _____.
   a. its members concentrate on working with outsiders
   b. it follows a rigorous chanting schedule
   c. its members value solitude

B. *Listen to each sentence. In the blank, write the letter of the definition or synonym that best completes the sentence.*

_____ 1.   a. widespread

_____ 2.   b. busy and full of activity

_____ 3.   c. eventually

_____ 4.   d. something that comes from God

_____ 5.   e. search

_____ 6.   f. eating little or no food for special reasons

C. *Listen to the sentences. Complete the restatement of each sentence below with the appropriate word or expression from the list.*

refrain from   caught on   pull back   took on   trace back   foster

1. Staying in a monastery may _____ spiritual development.

2. They _____ doing some things.

3. They can _____ their origins thousands of years.

4. They want to _____ from hectic lives.

5. It _____ the work when the need became apparent.

6. The chants _____ everywhere.

D. *Listen to the words. Pay attention to the vowel alternations of the underlined letters.*

a. div<u>i</u>ne /ay/   div<u>i</u>nity /ɪ/
b. gr<u>a</u>teful /ey/   gr<u>a</u>titude /æ/
c. h<u>ea</u>l /iy/   h<u>ea</u>lth /ɛ/
d. f<u>ai</u>th /ey/   f<u>ai</u>thful /ey/
   (no vowel alternation)

Now listen to these sentences. Write the letter of the vowel alternation you hear.

_____ 1.
_____ 2.
_____ 3.
_____ 4.
_____ 5.

E. *Listen to the sentences. Complete the restatement of each sentence below with **little, a little, few,** or **a few**.*

1. There is usually _____ movement.

2. _____ are allowed.

3. They have _____ trust.

4. They eat _____ food.

5. He enjoyed visiting _____ monasteries.

6. It was able to earn _____ money.

7. Before this, _____ people had heard of it.

TEST 2

You have the opportunity to spend seven days at a monastery. Think about the type of monastery where you would like to spend this time. What aspects of monastery life would you like to experience?

Talk to your partner, small group, or class about the type of monastery you would like to visit and the aspects of monastery life that you would like to experience. Use appropriate vocabulary from the unit and correct count and non-count nouns.

Achievement Tests
Unit 7

Name: _____

Date: _____

TEST 1

A. ☐1 *Listen to the excerpt. Mark the sentences **T** (true) or **F** (false).*

_____ **1.** The speaker is an employer.

_____ **2.** The speaker does not trust the people who work at his business.

_____ **3.** Trusting his employees gives the speaker satisfaction.

☐2 *Listen to the excerpt again. Circle the answer that best completes each sentence.*

1. According to the speaker, an employer should _____.
   a. tell his employees what is right and wrong
   b. watch his employees closely
   c. let his employees decide what is right and wrong

2. According to the speaker, being "Big Brother" is _____.
   a. an effective management strategy
   b. an ineffective management strategy
   c. neither effective nor ineffective

3. When the speaker says "go that extra mile," he means _____.
   a. exercising by running an extra mile
   b. getting satisfaction and rewards
   c. working extra hard

B. *Listen to each sentence. In the blank, write the letter of the synonym or definition that best completes the sentence.*

_____ **1.**   **a.** evil

_____ **2.**   **b.** insult

_____ **3.**   **c.** listen to secretly

_____ **4.**   **d.** unpredictably, without our choosing

_____ **5.**   **e.** insulting comments about a person's race

_____ **6.**   **f.** prevent

C. *Listen to the sentences. Complete the restatement of each sentence below with the appropriate expression from the list.*

is all well and good	keep tabs on	cheap shot
leave . . . at the door	fine line	think twice about

1. There is a _____.

2. They dislike having someone _____ them.

3. They feel that this is a _____.

4. It _____, but their employers should trust them.

5. They would _____ working for such a company.

6. They should not have to _____ their privacy

  _____.

D. *Listen to the sentences. Put a stress mark (') over the stressed syllable of each word below.*

1. conduct　　　3. present　　　5. insult
2. suspect　　　4. object

E. *Listen to the sentences. Complete the restatement of each sentence below with either the gerund or the infinitive form of the appropriate verb in the list.*

perform　videotape　interview　hire　arrive　question　identify

1. Joe Smith remembers _____ Jane.

2. Joe hired Jane, but he soon began _____ his decision.

3. It became her habit _____ late to work.

4. Then she stopped _____ the special tasks he requested.

5. Joe regretted _____ her.

6. Joe's company later decided _____ the job interviews so that managers could review them.

7. Now a team of executives tries _____ any undesirable traits.

TEST 2

You have a job where you work at a computer. You are very upset because you have just discovered that your boss has been monitoring everything you do on the computer. Your employer has also been using hidden surveillance cameras to observe you at work. You think your employer's actions are wrong.

Make an argument against your employer's actions. Use appropriate gerunds and infinitives in your argument. Tell your argument to your partner, small group, or class.

Achievement Tests
Unit 8

Name: _____

Date: _____

TEST 1

A. **1** *Listen to the excerpt. Mark the sentences **T** (true) or **F** (false).*

_____ 1. According to the speaker, the Red Cross believes that war can be abolished.

_____ 2. The Red Cross equates war with barbarism.

_____ 3. According to the speaker, war is sometimes desirable.

2 *Listen to the excerpt again. Circle the answer that best completes each sentence.*

1. According to the speaker, oppressed groups _____.
   a. should never use war to free themselves
   b. use barbarism in war
   c. sometimes must use war to free themselves

2. A rule that the Red Cross does NOT try to enforce is: _____.
   a. Don't shoot prisoners
   b. Don't kill people
   c. Don't make war on noncombatants

3. According to the speaker, it is important to distinguish between _____.
   a. oppression and war
   b. ethnic groups
   c. war and barbarism

B. *Listen to each sentence. In the blank, write the letter of the synonym or definition that best completes the sentence.*

_____ 1.	**a.** control
_____ 2.	**b.** communicate widely
_____ 3.	**c.** cruel and extremely violent behavior
_____ 4.	**d.** likely to explode, tense
_____ 5.	**e.** rules
_____ 6.	**f.** last for a long time

C. *Listen to each sentence. From the context, underline the correct word in each pair of words below.*

        1. a. affect   **b.** effect

        2. a. advice   **b.** advise

        3. a. assure   **b.** ensure

        4. a. assure   **b.** ensure

        5. a. council   **b.** counsel

        6. a. eminent   **b.** imminent

        7. a. accept   **b.** except

        8. a. access   **b.** excess

 D. *Listen to the words. Pay attention to the vowel pattern in the following pairs of words.*

        a. cup / ə /   cup / ə /

        b. cap / æ /   cap / æ /

        c. cup / ə /   cop / ɑ /

        d. cup / ə /   cap / æ /

        e. cap / æ /   cup / ə /

        (no vowel alternation)

Now listen to these sentences. Write the letter of the vowel pattern you hear.

      _____ **1.**

      _____ **2.**

      _____ **3.**

      _____ **4.**

      _____ **5.**

E. *Listen to the sentences. Change each sentence from direct to indirect speech.*

1. Margaret warned her commander _____

    _____

2. The public affairs officer told reporters _____

    _____

3. The prisoner of war asked one of the guards _____

    _____

4. The interviewer asked _____

    _____

5. Michael Ignatieff said _____

    _____

TEST 2

Make a public service announcement (PSA) about the dangers of war, guns, drugs, or alcohol. Use a brochure, poster, or handout to support your announcement.

Tell your public service announcement to your partner, small group, or class. In your PSA, use both direct and indirect speech from your visual aid or from experts.

TEST 1

A. ☐1 *Listen to the excerpt. Mark the sentences **T** (true) or **F** (false).*

_____ **1.** Children are born with mathematical ability.

_____ **2.** Exposure to music helped preschoolers with their spatial reasoning skills.

☐2 *Listen to the excerpt again. Circle the answer that best completes each sentence.*

1. The speaker describes music as _____.

    a. not very logical
    b. highly mathematical
    c. geometric

2. Preschoolers were taught _____.

    a. to solve mazes
    b. to copy geometric shapes
    c. singing and piano

3. The wiring for mathematics and music is located _____.

    a. on the right side of the brain
    b. on the left side of the brain
    c. at the base of the brain

B. *Listen to each sentence. In the blank, write the letter of the definition or synonym that best completes the sentence.*

_____ **1.**	**a.** an outstanding feature
_____ **2.**	**b.** in a particular order
_____ **3.**	**c.** improve
_____ **4.**	**d.** emphasize
_____ **5.**	**e.** complete and varied
_____ **6.**	**f.** the ability to understand general concepts

C. *Listen to each sentence. Circle the letter of the sentence below that is similar in meaning to the sentence you hear.*

1. **a.** They blow up people who try to help them.
   b. They blow up at people who try to help them.

2. **a.** They are afraid that they're going to blow it in math.
   b. They are afraid that they are going to blow up at math.

3. **a.** Parents worry that their children will be scarred by failure.
   b. Parents worry that their children will be orchestrated by failure.

4. **a.** It can help children blow up at their math problems.
   b. It can help children attack their math problems.

5. **a.** They are interested in the wiring for various activities.
   b. They are interested in the windows for various activities.

6. **a.** They have orchestrated scientific experiments.
   b. They have attacked scientific experiments.

7. **a.** They have opened up wiring for new kinds of school curricula.
   b. They have opened up windows for new kinds of school curricula.

8. **a.** They deserve a big hand.
   b. They deserve big hands.

 D. *Listen to the sentences. Each sentence contains a repeated phrase. In each blank, write the letter of one of the rules below.*

a. Join the final consonant and vowel.

b. Hold one long consonant.

c. Keep the final consonant short, hold it, and immediately say the next word.

_____ 1. mathematical ability

_____ 2. standardized tests

_____ 3. music classes

_____ 4. government funding

E. *Listen to the sentences. Complete the restatement of each sentence below with the appropriate form of the verbs in the list. Use active or passive forms.*

offer   indicate   convince   include   give   get   improve

1. Some educators _____ that the creative arts have a positive effect.

2. New research _____ new connections.

3. Some children _____ music lessons.

4. Their math skills _____ .

5. The sooner children _____ such an opportunity, the better.

6. Special programs _____ .

7. They _____ music, drama, and art.

TEST 2

Make a list of subjects that children study in school. Include a variety of subjects, such as math, physical education, and painting.

Tell your partner, small group, or class which subject is the most important and which subject is the least important for children to study. Make strong arguments by using the active voice of the verbs.

Achievement Tests
Unit 10

Name: _____

Date: _____

TEST 1

A. ☐1 *Listen to the excerpt. Mark the sentences **T** (true) or **F** (false).*

_____ **1.** Broadcasters support the V-chip/ratings system.

_____ **2.** Broadcasters trust the public to use the V-chip.

_____ **3.** Supporters of freedom of speech feel that the V-chip/ratings system is censorship.

☐2 *Listen to the excerpt again. Circle the answer that best completes each sentence.*

1. Broadcasters think the public _____.

   a. can be trusted to use the V-chip consistently
   b. is hypocritical
   c. wants less sex and violence on TV

2. The Telecommunications Act _____.

   a. ordered the establishment of a TV ratings system
   b. ordered broadcasters to control their own programming
   c. ordered the establishment of the V-chip system

3. The FCC (Federal Communications Commission) can _____.

   a. control the protests of free speech supporters
   b. set up its own ratings system
   c. reject the Telecommunications Act

B. *Listen to each sentence. In the blank, write the letter of the definition or synonym that best completes the sentence.*

_____ **1.**   **a.** not forced

_____ **2.**   **b.** promised

_____ **3.**   **c.** contradictory

_____ **4.**   **d.** perfect solution, cure-all

_____ **5.**   **e.** disturbing

_____ **6.**   **f.** cancel out

_____ **7.**   **g.** something that looks enjoyable because it is not allowed

C. *Listen to each sentence. Circle the letter of the sentence below that is similar in meaning to the sentence you hear.*

1. **a.** They are the basic staple of programming.
   b. They are special and unique.

2. **a.** These parents feel it is good and healthy.
   b. These parents are annoyed and sickened by it.

3. **a.** They don't believe that watching violent TV shows leads to more violent behavior.
   b. They believe that watching violent TV shows leads to violent behavior.

4. **a.** Government action does not include censorship.
   b. Government action is grouped with censorship.

5. **a.** These people never want to do it.
   b. These people almost always want to do it.

6. **a.** They feel that the programs are morally good and healthy.
   b. They feel that the programs are of poor quality.

7. **a.** They say that there is enough morally good and healthy programming.
   b. They say that there is mostly poor-quality programming.

 D. *Listen to the sentences. Underline the phrasal verbs and put a stress mark (') over the stressed word.*

1. Some families are pledging to <u>turn óff</u> their television sets for a month.

2. By not being glued to the TV set, the Smith family gains the opportunity to try out new activities.

3. The children set up a jigsaw puzzle on the kitchen table, and the whole family has been working on it each evening after dinner.

4. Mr. and Mrs. Smith started completing some projects they've been putting off for a long time.

E. *Listen to each conversation. Circle the letter of the sentence below that restates the second speaker's response.*

1. **a.** No, they shouldn't have because I told them not to.
   b. No, they couldn't have because we have the V-chip.

2. **a.** You may be able to.
   b. You ought to be able to.

3. **a.** They shouldn't.
   b. They can't.

4. **a.** It might have.
   b. It must have.

5. **a.** They couldn't have.
   b. They might not have.

6. **a.** That may be.
   b. That must be.

TEST 2

Mr. and Mrs. Green permit their eleven-year-old daughter and twelve-year-old son to watch television programs that include sex and violence. They do not think that violence or sex on television harms children.

Tell your partner, small group, or class what advice you would give to the Greens. Use modals.

Achievement Tests
Test 1 Audioscript

UNIT 1

A

1 *Listen to the excerpt. Mark the sentences **T** (true) or **F** (false).*

David Alpern: Seriously, though, just last week we reported on research suggesting that all the multitasking may actually make our brains work better and faster producing as it's been reported a world-wide increase in IQ up to 20 points and more in recent decades. Can you see any benefit in all these mental gymnastics we now have to go through?

David Brooks: Yeah, I, I, I don't think we're becoming a race of global idiots, uh, but I think certain skills are enhanced and certain are not. You know the ability to make fast decisions, to answer a dozen e-mails in five minutes, uh to fill out maybe big SAT type tests. That's enhanced. But creativity is something that happens slowly. It happens when your brain is just noodling around, just playing. When it puts together ideas which you hadn't thought of or maybe you have time say to read a book. You are a businessperson but you have time to read a book about history or time to read a book about a philosopher and something that happened long ago or something or some idea somebody thought of long ago. Actually, you know, it occurs to you that you can think of your own business in that way, and so it's this mixture of unrelated ideas ah that feeds your productivity, feeds your creativity and if your mind is disciplined to answer every e-mail, then you don't have time for that playful noodling. You don't have time for those unexpected conjunctions so I think maybe we're getting smarter in some senses but I think it is a threat to our creativity and to our reflection.

2 *Listen to the excerpt again. Circle the answer that best completes each sentence.*

B

Listen to each sentence. In the blank, write the letter of the definition or synonym that best completes the sentence.

1. Many people enjoy surfing the Internet. *Internet surfing* is . . .
2. Some people become compulsive about using the Internet. *Compulsive* means . . .
3. When people see a doctor, they present with a certain problem. *Present with* means . . .
4. Some people seek therapy for their addiction problems. *Therapy* is . . .
5. Some people with problems find help in support groups. *Support groups* are . . .

C

Listen to each statement. Circle the letter of the sentence with a similar meaning.

1. Today many people are turning into workaholics.
2. Even on vacation, some people have to know what's going on in the office.
3. These people don't use their vacations to enhance their personal lives.
4. Workaholics might call the office just to noodle around with co-workers about some project that they're working on.
5. In some workplaces, people are required to multitask because there are not enough employees to do all the jobs that need to be done.
6. These people are bombarded with one task after another.
7. People may feel overwhelmed by all the tasks they must complete at work.

D

Listen to the sentences. Circle the word that is highlighted in each sentence.

1. My roommate spends *hours* on the Internet every day.
2. When does he do his *homework?*
3. That's the problem—he *doesn't.*
4. Then he's *not* going to pass his classes.
5. I know, but all *he* cares about is his computer.

E

Listen to the first part of each exchange. Complete each exchange with an appropriate short-answer wish statement.

1. Is your friend addicted to the computer?
2. Will he agree to get some therapy?
3. Did you know before this that a person could become addicted to computers?
4. Did you try talking with him about the problem?
5. Can I do something to help?

UNIT 2

A

1 *Listen to the excerpt. Mark the sentences **T** (true) or **F** (false).*

Terri Gross: You know, this whole sense of, like, it's going to be a new town, but we are going to do it with a sense of nostalgia for the past so nothing can be designed past what existed in the 1940s—it seems—it just seems a little contradictory, and some of the designs from the

1940s didn't really transfer that well into the 90s like, a lot of the houses had porches.

Douglas Franz: . . . what Disney expected with these front porches, what the planners envisioned was it would create a front porch culture, that people would be out on their porches talking to their neighbors next door and to people walking down the street or people riding their bikes, and there would be this culture that, you know, either existed or existed in somebody's imagination, you know 30, 40, 50 years ago. But that really has been one of the failures that we observed during our two years in Celebration, and the people don't spend very much time at all on their front porches. There are a couple things going on. One is it's central Florida, and it's hotter than hell a good part of the year, and sitting on your front porch, even if you have a fan going, can be a very uncomfortable thing. People prefer to be inside in the air conditioning.

2 *Listen to the excerpt again. Read the questions and circle the best answer.*

B _____

Listen to each sentence. Circle the letter of the sentence below that is most similar in meaning to the sentence you hear.

1. The downtown area of the city has a vibrant nightlife.
2. Utopian societies are sometimes bothered by the scrutiny of outsiders.
3. Some new urban developments attempt to nurture a sense of community.
4. Sometimes people feel a sense of nostalgia for the past.
5. To create a sense of community is a laudable goal.
6. A well-planned community includes access to open spaces.
7. After Celebration was built, the media assessed how the community was doing.
8. Some residents of Celebration felt that the media scrutiny was callous.

C _____

Listen to each sentence. In the blank, write the letter of the definition or synonym that best completes the sentence.

1. Sometimes people become so busy working to make ends meet that they don't have time to enjoy themselves. To *make ends meet* means . . .
2. Some of these people become so burned out on their busy lives that they wish that they could move to a utopia. *Burned out* means . . .
3. However, even in utopia people have to live by certain rules. To *live by* rules means . . .
4. It will be interesting to see how some of the new attempts at utopian societies play out. *Play out* means . . .

D _____

*Listen to the sentences. Each sentence contains **as, has, is,** or **-es,** pronounced /əz/. Circle the one you hear in each sentence.*

1. This town is the perfect place to live.
2. The town has been carefully planned.
3. They built that house as a model.
4. A sense of community is important.
5. People sit on their porches in the summer.

E _____

Imagine that you are being interviewed about your utopian community. Listen to each question. Write an answer using the cues provided. Add words where necessary.

1. How should people contact you for information about your utopian community?
2. What is one of your rules?
3. What about the roof color?
4. What if a resident wants to build a fence?
5. What will the lawns look like?
6. What should people plant on their lawns?
7. What if someone doesn't like these rules?

UNIT 3

A _____

1 *Listen to the excerpt. Mark the sentences **T** (true) or **F** (false).*

I'm Julie Danis with "Tales from the Workplace."

Arriving at the office after a visit to the eye doctor with no diagnosis for my blurred vision, I was in a grouchy mood. "No time to be cranky," a co-worker said, "we have a project due." "Besides," she continued, "now you have a prescription to skip the mascara and rest your eyes, every two hours."

She'd done it again, I realized. She had made lemonade out of lemons. We all know people like this. They find the silver lining inside the darkest cloud . . . all the time . . . without fail . . . driving others to distraction with their "find the bright side" philosophy. . . .

This optimistic outlook does have its merits. . . .

But don't get carried away. Nothing will take away the ache in your mouth or fill the void in your pocketbook from two root canals, not covered by your company's health plan.

So, the next time someone says, "You can't cry over something that can't cry over you," assert yourself in the face of their sunny-side-up point of view. State firmly, "Yes I can, and I plan to do just that." Then go suck on some lemons and feel better in your own way. . . .

2 *Listen to the excerpt again. Circle the answer that best completes each sentence.*

B

Listen to the sentences. Complete the restatement of each sentence below with the appropriate definition or synonym from the list.

1. Some people who seem to act as if they think they're better than you are really just very shy.
2. Most shy people don't want to keep themselves separate from others, but they often don't know how to begin conversations.
3. For example, Mary wanted to be the life of the party, but she was not outgoing.
4. Instead, when Mary was in a large group, she became very quiet, only speaking when she was asked a direct question.
5. Her shyness began to badly affect other parts of her life.
6. Mary began to feel afraid all the time. She could not even leave the house each day.
7. Mary spoke by telephone with a therapist, and he helped her realize that her ideas were important enough to express.
8. She began to attend a support group, where she met a friend with whom she had so much in common that to this day they are still best friends.

C

Listen to each sentence. In the blank, write the letter of the definition or synonym that best completes the sentence.

1. I used to consider myself as alone in the world. *Consider* means . . .
2. I felt empty inside, with nothing to stop the emptiness. To *stop the emptiness* is to . . .
3. I was afraid to attend the first support group meeting, but you were able to get people socializing by introducing me to everyone right away. To *get people socializing* is to . . .
4. You're able to encourage even the quietest people. *Encourage* means . . .
5. Thanks to you and the group, my point of view on life has changed. *Point of view* means . . .
6. First of all, I learned that I'm not the only one who is shy in large groups of people. *First of all* means . . .
7. Besides, I don't have to let shyness label me as a person without merit. *Label* means . . .
8. In fact, I may end up studying for a career as a therapist! *End up* means . . .

D

Listen to each sentence. Circle the letter of the one you hear.

1. Her co-worker said she's got a project to finish.
2. "My co-worker," says Julie, "makes lemonade out of lemons."
3. You need to see the therapist who is an expert on shyness.

E

Listen to each pair of sentences. The second sentence of each pair is in the list. Use the list to make adjective clauses and complete the sentences. Add commas where necessary.

1. Mary began to attend support group meetings. She had a problem with chronic shyness.
2. Mary met another woman. This woman's interests were the same as hers.
3. Mary enjoyed attending the meetings. She met other shy people there.
4. Mary never missed her meetings. She found the meetings very helpful.
5. Mary continued to attend the meetings and meet with her therapist. Both of these helped her.
6. Mary looked forward to a time. She would feel more confident at that time.

UNIT 4

A

1 Listen to the excerpt. Mark the sentences *T* (true) or *F* (false).

Malcolm Gladwell: Well, in New York we had the perfect test case of that idea. It starts in the subway. You know, in the early 80s they decided to clean up the subway. Well, how did they do it? The subway was a complete mess, right? It was . . . crime rates were going through the roof. They bring in a man who is a big a disciple of this idea, of broken windows, and what does he do? Well, the first thing he does is he picks up all the litter. The second thing he does is he cleans up the graffiti, and the third thing he does is he says from now on, no one will ever jump a turnstile in a New York City subway station again. He puts cops by the turnstiles and if someone jumps, he arrests them. Everybody said he was crazy, but you've got a subway system where people are killing, and robbing, and assaulting and raping each other and what do you do? You go after the two kinds of criminality that, the only two kinds of criminality that in fact don't hurt anybody else, right? Turnstile jumping and graffiti, you know, littering and graffiti but it turns out that those were tipping points. Once they put those three changes in place, the subway starts to come around really quite dramatically.

2 Listen to the excerpt again. Circle the answer that best completes each sentence.

B

Listen to each sentence. In the blank, write the lettter of the definition or synonym that best completes the sentence.

1. A person who knows a lot about a particular subject and loves to share his knowledge is . . .
2. A large number of cases of an infectious disease occurring at the same time is known as . . .

3. When there is a serious disease or a complex problem, it is important to get to the cause or source, in other words, to find . . .

4. When someone is very determined to do something, we can say that person is . . .

5. The candidate persuaded many people to vote for her—that is, she . . .

6. How much income will the movie produce? That is, how much money will it . . .

7. When an idea or trend spreads because people tell other people, it is called . . .

C

Listen to the sentences. Complete the restatement of each sentence below with the appropriate word or expression from the list.

1. When Rachel Carson's book *Silent Spring* was published, it quickly became a best-seller.

2. She found that DDT accumulated in the tissues of animals all the way up the food chain, including humans.

3. When Rachel Carson suggested that DDT not be used, she was going against the usual way of doing things.

4. Based on Rachel Carson's conclusions, a government investigation began into the effects of DDT.

5. At first, chemical companies did not want DDT to be banned. They hoped to be able to simply be more careful in their use of DDT.

6. Rachel Carson's ideas created a movement of people that brought about many other environmentally conscious changes.

7. Her ideas were just the beginning of many environmentally conscious government decisions that followed.

D

Listen to the words. Put a stress mark (') over the stressed syllable in each word.

1. transmission
2. chaotic
3. sensitivity
4. theoretical
5. influential

E

Listen to the sentences about Rachel Carson's Silent Spring. *Complete each sentence below with* **so** *or* **such** *and the appropriate word or phrase from the list.*

1. When Rachel Carson decided to write an article about the dangers of DDT, magazine publishers refused to publish the article because they were afraid of losing advertisers.

2. Rachel Carson decided to write the book *Silent Spring* because she felt that her message was important.

3. After the book was published, some people in the chemical industry attacked Rachel Carson personally and questioned her conclusions because they were very angry.

4. However, respected experts supported her because she had done very careful research.

5. The chemical was finally banned because the government was convinced of the harmful effects of DDT.

UNIT 5

A

1 *Listen to the excerpt. Mark the sentences* **T** *(true) or* **F** *(false).*

Listen to my tale of a true tragedy that occurred in Hong Kong several years ago. Most people say Bruce Lee, the famous kung fu actor, shouldn't have bought the house in the valley. The wind in the valley can destroy the ch'i. People didn't understand why he chose that particular area since the wealthy actor could've lived anywhere in Hong Kong. Rumor has it, though, that in order to change his feng shui, he put a mirror on a tree in the backyard. This might've worked if there hadn't been an accident.

The tree was destroyed in a storm, and he never replaced the tree or the mirror. If he had, most people say he wouldn't have died. It is said that the unfavorable feng shui must've caused his death. Replacing the tree and the mirror immediately could've saved his life.

2 *Listen to the excerpt again. Circle the answer that best completes each sentence.*

B

Listen to each sentence. In the blank, write the letter of the definition or synonym that best completes the sentence.

1. Speakers sometimes tell anecdotes to get their listeners' attention. An *anecdote* is . . .

2. People who are not familiar with a concept may frown upon it because they don't like new ideas. To *frown upon* something is to . . .

3. Some reporters have been covering news stories for so long that they are hard-bitten. *Hard-bitten* means . . .

4. These hard-bitten reporters may listen skeptically when someone explains a concept that is not scientifically proven. To listen *skeptically* is to listen . . .

5. Instead of trying to prove some ideas scientifically, people who believe in the ideas may say that we should sense the truth. To *sense* is to . . .

6. Some ideas that cannot be explained scientifically are described as transcendent. *Transcendent* means . . .

C

Listen to the sentences. Complete the restatement of each sentence below with the appropriate expression from the list.

1. Recently, my friend convinced me to change around the furniture in my bedroom.
2. I was involved in final exams, so at first I really didn't want to do it.
3. "Look," my friend said to me, "your academic career is not going to succeed or fail if you take a short break to improve your living space."
4. I was worried. Sometimes my friend doesn't understand that exams really frighten me!
5. Finally, I said to myself, "I guess it can do no harm to take a little break."
6. For a long time, I had been afraid to take action, so my room looked the same as it did when I first moved into it.
7. Once we started, I really became interested in changing everything around. Soon my room looked like a new place.
8. Thanks to my friend, my room is a great place to study now. And I have been able to compensate for my busy exam schedule by studying more now in my new room.

D

Listen to the sentences. Fill in the blanks with the modal perfect forms.

1. If my friend hadn't convinced me, I wouldn't have changed my room around.
2. I probably should have studied that night, but I wanted to take a break.
3. Without my friend's help, I couldn't have made the changes.
4. My friend must have done this type of thing before.
5. I can't believe how good my room looks! I should have done this a long time ago!

E

Listen to each pair of sentences. The second sentence contains a discourse connector. In the blank for each sentence, write the correct type of discourse connector from the list.

1. Feng shui has recently become popular in the West. Consequently, some people are using it in their homes and businesses.
2. Feng shui experts consider the shape, size, and location of objects. Moreover, they consider the energy within the business.
3. If ch'i flows smoothly, things will go well for people. On the other hand, if ch'i is blocked, things may go badly.
4. Some farmers in the Gobi Desert and Mongolia built their huts facing north. As a result, their homes were battered by the wind and dust.
5. Feng shui practitioners recommend *not* putting mirrors in a bedroom. However, mirrors can work well in other rooms.

UNIT 6

A

1 *Listen to the excerpt. Mark the sentences **T** (true) or **F** (false).*

William Claassen: . . . Although Wat Tham Krabat is part of this forest monastic tradition, it was different in the sense that they were working on issues that were outside of the monastery. They had taken on efforts of working with AIDS patients and also providing assistance with Hmong villagers who were refugees out of Laos who had begun gathering in that area where the monastery was located. So, actually, a great deal of their time was spent in this work, the AIDS work, and also the work with the refugees, which, uh, created a little different situation in terms of their daily schedule, in terms of how rigorous their chanting schedule was, in terms of the solitude of the community because there were a lot of people coming in, children as well as adults, as well as Westerners, coming in to view this program for the AIDS patients, also for drug addicts. They also worked in that area. So, there was a lot of movement in and out of the community, which made it a different situation than what I experienced in other forest monasteries.

2 *Listen to the excerpt again. Circle the answer that best completes each sentence.*

B

Listen to each sentence. In the blank, write the letter of the definition or synonym that best completes the sentence.

1. The monastery was very hectic. *Hectic* means . . .
2. Monks believe that their work is divine. *Divine* means . . .
3. Some people choose a life of simplicity because materialism is so pervasive. *Pervasive* means . . .
4. Some monks engage in fasting. *Fasting* is . . .
5. William Claassen thought of his investigation of monasteries as not only a fact-finding journey but also a spiritual quest. A *quest* is a kind of . . .
6. Claassen found that some monasteries did not remain the same but changed over time because of outside pressures. *Over time* means . . .

C

Listen to the sentences. Complete the restatement of each sentence below with the appropriate word or expression from the list.

1. Staying in a monastery may *help* some people *develop* their spiritual lives.
2. The monastic life often means that members *do not do* some things that they want to do.
3. Some monasteries *found their origins* thousands of years ago.
4. People sometimes enter monasteries because they want to *retreat* from hectic daily lives.

5. Wat Tham Krabat monastery *started* work with AIDS patients and refugees when that need became apparent.

6. One monastery recorded an album of Gregorian chants that *became popular* around the world.

D _____

Listen to the words. Pay attention to the vowel alternations of the underlined letters.

a. divine—divinity
b. grateful—gratitude
c. heal—health
d. faith—faithful

Now listen to these sentences. Write the letter of the vowel alternation you hear.

1. I enjoy being out in nature. I love the natural world. *Nature—natural.*
2. My faith is important to me. I want to be faithful to my beliefs. *Faith—faithful.*
3. I would enjoy the monastic life. I would like to live in a monastery. *Life—live.*
4. The monastic life would please me. The monastic life would give me great pleasure. *Please—pleasure.*
5. The material world is not always a sane place. A monastic lifestyle would bring me sanity. *Sane—sanity.*

E _____

*Listen to the sentences. Complete the restatement of each sentence below with **little, a little, few,** or **a few**.*

1. Some monastic communities value solitude, so not very many people move in or out.
2. These monasteries do not allow many visitors.
3. Visitors are considered interruptions, and the monks do not trust them.
4. People who are fasting do not eat because they want to concentrate on their spiritual lives.
5. Whenever he had an opportunity, William Claassen enjoyed visiting some monasteries.
6. A monastery in Spain was able to earn some money to help pay its day-to-day expenses by selling the chant album.
7. Not very many people had heard of the monastery of Santo Domingo before the chant album, but now the monastery is world-famous.

UNIT 7

A _____

1 *Listen to the excerpt. Mark the sentences **T** (true) or **F** (false).*

I own a small data-processing company in which I employ about eight to ten workers. The point I want to make has to do with trust. Listen, I know it's possible to force people to be 100 percent efficient. But when you do that you lose morale, confidence, trust. I let my

employees use our equipment, computers, make personal phone calls, whatever. They are more than welcome to decide what is right and wrong. You can't run a company by just issuing orders to robots and watching them like Big Brother. You have to trust people, respect them, and give them a little freedom. Also, as far as phone calls and all that go, I want my people to call home and check on their children, and know their children are okay, because then they can refocus on the job . . . and their work is better. As a result, I have dedicated employees who are willing to go that extra mile . . . to show up at work smiling. I get more satisfaction and rewards by trusting my employees than by suspecting them of doing something wrong.

2 *Listen to the excerpt again. Circle the answer that best completes each sentence.*

B _____

Listen to each sentence. In the blank, write the letter of the synonym or definition that best completes the sentence.

1. When my employer watches my every move, it demeans me. To *demean* is to . . .
2. Do surveillance cameras really deter theft? To *deter* is to . . .
3. Is it immoral to eavesdrop on other people? To *eavesdrop* is to . . .
4. Racial slurs are also immoral. *Racial slurs* are . . .
5. Big Brother in the workplace is a sinister concept. *Sinister* means . . .
6. Employee monitoring should not be done willy-nilly. To do something *willy-nilly* means to do it . . .

C _____

Listen to the sentences. Complete the restatement of each sentence below with the appropriate expression from the list.

1. There is an *unclear distinction* between monitoring productivity and invading people's privacy.
2. Some employees dislike having their employer *carefully* observe their phone calls and e-mail.
3. These employees feel that this "spying" is an *unfair attack* by the employer.
4. They also believe that it *is satisfactory* for their employers to expect quality work, but that their employers should trust them to do their jobs well.
5. Before working for a company that watches its employees very closely, such people would *consider the problems* with it.
6. These people think that when they walk into the workplace, they should not have to *forget about* their privacy.

D _____

Listen to the sentences. Put a stress mark (') over the stressed syllable of each word below.

1. Employers may be concerned about the conduct of their employees on the phone. *Conduct.*

2. Employers may suspect their employees of making personal calls. *Suspect.*
3. Recording phone calls may present a problem. *Present.*
4. Employees often object to having their calls monitored. *Object.*
5. Employees feel that having their calls monitored is an insult. *Insult.*

E

Listen to the sentences. Complete the restatement of each sentence below with either the gerund or the infinitive form of the appropriate verb in the list.

1. I'm Joe Smith, a manager at XYZ Corporation. I remember when I talked to one employee, Jane, about a job.
2. I hired Jane, but I began to doubt the decision soon afterward.
3. She soon started coming late to work every day.
4. Then she wouldn't do the special tasks I requested.
5. I was sorry that I'd given her a job.
6. My company made the decision to have the job interviews recorded so that they could be reviewed.
7. Now a team of executives watches the video to look for any negative characteristics.

UNIT 8

A

1 *Listen to the excerpt. Mark the sentences T (true) or F (false).*

Michael Ignatieff: . . . I grew up in the anti-war culture of my generation. . . . I think what I discovered in the Red Cross's approach is an alternative ethic, which is that, you know, you cannot abolish war, you can't do without war. And war in fact is a natural, necessary, and sometimes, dare I say it, even desirable way to solve certain social conflicts between ethnic groups. Oppressed groups sometimes can only use war to free themselves. Well, if that's the case, if we can't abolish war from human culture, then we'd better find some way to tame it.

And that's the ethic that the Red Cross lives by, and I think the simple rules that the Red Cross tries to enforce, which is, you don't shoot prisoners, you don't make war on noncombatants, you try and stay away from civilian targets, you kill people, you don't torture or degrade their bodies. You know, just very, very simple rules of humanity are an important addition to civilization. And there is no necessary reason . . . I suppose that this is what I've learned . . . to equate war with barbarism. There's a distinction between war and barbarism. And we should keep to that distinction and struggle to ensure it, and that's what the Red Cross tries to do.

2 *Listen to the excerpt again. Circle the answer that best completes each sentence.*

B

Listen to each sentence. In the blank, write the letter of the synonym or definition that best completes the sentence.

1. Nowadays, war is sometimes considered to be nothing but barbarism and savagery. *Savagery* is . . .
2. The Geneva Convention consists of codes. *Codes* are . . .
3. The Red Cross disseminates safety information to people in dangerous situations. To *disseminate* is to . . .
4. When world events cause great tension, people hope that peace will prevail. To *prevail* is to . . .
5. In a warrior tradition, fighters learned not to unleash their aggression but to restrain themselves. To *restrain* means to . . .
6. The warriors trained hard to learn control in volatile situations. *Volatile* means . . .

C

Listen to each sentence. From the context, underline the correct word in each pair of words below.

1. Crisis situations often *affect* entire communities.
2. Red Cross volunteers *advise* disaster victims where to get help.
3. Volunteers often *assure* frightened people that they are there to help them.
4. The volunteers *ensure* that victims receive much-needed food and water.
5. Volunteers also *counsel* people about safety measures.
6. Whenever danger is *imminent*, Red Cross volunteers are ready to help.
7. Generally, people are happy to *accept* the help of the Red Cross volunteers.
8. Sometimes volunteers have no *access* to disaster victims because roads are destroyed or blocked.

D

Listen to the words. Pay attention to the vowel pattern in the following pairs of words.

a. cup—cup
b. cap—cap
c. cup—cop
d. cup—cap
e. cap—cup

Now listen to these sentences. Write the letter of the vowel pattern you hear.

1. People disagree on how to spend government funds. *Government funds.*
2. Modern cultural values are different from those of our ancestors. *Cultural values.*
3. Today, some people believe that all war is a savage act. *Savage act.*
4. Some recent decisions to fight have caused public controversy. *Public controversy.*
5. Government decisions may be met by a widespread lack of trust. *Lack trust.*

Listen to the sentences. Change each sentence from direct to indirect speech.

1. Margaret warned her commander, a man, "Don't treat me like a child."
2. The public affairs officer told reporters, "We have just lost twenty soldiers."
3. The prisoner of war asked the guard, "Can I send a birthday card to my daughter?"
4. The interviewer asked, "How is the Red Cross trying to educate people?"
5. Michael Ignatieff said, "I grew up in the anti-war culture of my generation."

UNIT 9

A

1 *Listen to the excerpt. Mark the sentences **T** (true) or **F** (false).*

Warren Levinson: I was fascinated by some of the research on music and the relationship to other kinds of reasoning, particularly mathematics. I had always assumed that musical talent and mathematics kind of went together because they had something to do with each other . . . um . . . in terms of filling puzzles . . . and in terms of . . . you have mathematics involved in setting out the beats to various kinds of music. . . .

Sharon Begley: That's right. Yes . . . music itself is highly mathematical, and that made some neuro-scientists think that somehow the patterns of firing in neural cells were similar, as in mathematical abilities and logical thinking and spatial reasoning. So what they did is give two-and three-year-olds—little preschoolers—lessons in singing and piano, and after several weeks of this, the children were much better at solving mazes on pieces of paper and copying geometric shapes, so it seems again that these circuits were sort of primed to be wired up, and music somehow did it.

WL: But it also turns out that they tend . . . the wiring for both of those things tend to be right next to each other. . . .

SB: They're in the same part of the brain . . . this old right side of the brain that we've heard about for years . . . yeah.

2 *Listen to the excerpt again. Circle the answer that best completes each sentence.*

B

Listen to each sentence. In the blank, write the letter of the definition or synonym that best completes the sentence.

1. Research shows that music lessons can enhance other skills. To *enhance* is to . . .
2. One skill that is enhanced by music lessons is *abstract reasoning*. *Abstract reasoning* is . . .
3. Music and math both involve sequential elements. *Sequential* means . . .

4. Subjects from the arts as well as basic subjects are part of a well-rounded education. *Well-rounded* means . . .
5. A well-rounded curriculum is the hallmark of a good education. A *hallmark* is . . .
6. Increases in test scores underscore the importance of the arts. To *underscore* is to . . .

C

Listen to each sentence. Circle the letter of the sentence below that is similar in meaning to the sentence you hear.

1. Sometimes children become so frustrated with their homework that they become angry with anyone who tries to help.
2. Some children are especially afraid that they're going to fail in math.
3. Parents are worried that their children will be permanently harmed by failure.
4. Learning music can help children approach their math problems more easily.
5. Scientists who study the brain are interested in the neural transmitters for various activities.
6. These scientists want to test the relationship between music and spatial reasoning, so they have carefully developed experiments.
7. Their observations have opened up opportunities for new types of school curricula.
8. Those who try to help children succeed deserve great applause.

D

Listen to the sentences. Each sentence contains a repeated phrase. In each blank, write the letter of one of the rules below.

1. Musical and mathematical ability are in the same part of the brain. *Mathematical ability.*
2. Children who take art classes tend to earn higher scores on standardized tests than those who do not. *Standardized tests.*
3. Music classes should be a part of every school's curriculum. *Music classes.*
4. School districts should receive government funding for classes in the arts. *Government funding.*

E

Listen to the sentences. Complete the restatement of each sentence below with the appropriate form of the verbs in the list. Use active or passive forms.

1. Some educators believe strongly that participation in the creative arts has a positive effect on children's ability to learn.
2. Recent research suggests new connections between music and math.
3. For example, some children are exposed to music lessons.
4. These children increase their skills in mathematics.

5. The sooner children receive such an opportunity, the more likely they are to succeed in other areas of learning.
6. As a result, special programs are provided by some school districts.
7. Among these special programs are music, drama, and art.

UNIT 10

A

[1] *Listen to the excerpt. Mark the sentences **T** (true) or **F** (false).*

Broadcasters feel that the V-chip/ratings system is only a quick technological fix. They worry that parents who use the V-chip will block out prime-time shows, profitable evening programs which serve as their bread-and-butter programming. Moreover, broadcasters don't trust the public to use the system. Even though parents say they want less sex and violence on TV, shows containing such scenes are often the most popular. Broadcasters think the public is hypocritical and doubt that any electronic blocking device or a ratings system will actually be used.

Supporters of freedom of speech, or First Amendment rights, are the loudest protesters against the V-chip/ratings system. They can't swallow the idea of blocking out certain programs. For them, this system falls under the category of censorship. In the Telecommunications Act, the government ordered the television industry to establish a ratings system. The law also ordered the television manufacturers to install blocking devices in all new sets. The FCC (Federal Communications Commission), a government agency, is responsible for approving the implementation of the V-chip/ratings system. It can reject the broadcasters' ratings system and set up its own. Free speech supporters feel that the government has ultimate power and control over what is shown on television. Therefore, they see this power as full-fledged censorship.

[2] *Listen to the excerpt again. Circle the answer that best completes each sentence.*

B

Listen to each sentence. In the blank, write the letter of the definition or synonym that best completes the sentence.

1. When his parents went out for dinner, the boy enjoyed the forbidden fruit of a violent movie. *Forbidden fruit* is . . .
2. None of his parents' advice could counteract the boy's attraction to the program. *Counteract* means . . .
3. The boy had pledged to turn off the television when a violent program came on. *Pledged* means . . .

4. The government's idea to solve the problem of TV violence with additional children's programming was not a panacea. A *panacea* is a . . .
5. It was obvious that the television executive was hypocritical when he approved the violent TV program but said he was against violence. *Hypocritical* means . . .
6. Some people find sexually explicit material to be offensive. *Offensive* means . . .
7. In some countries, TV rating systems are voluntary. *Voluntary* means . . .

C

Listen to each sentence. Circle the letter of the sentence below that is similar in meaning to the sentence you hear.

1. Prime-time programs are the bread-and-butter of television networks.
2. Many parents are disgusted by the sex and violence that they see on TV.
3. Some people can't swallow the idea that watching violent TV shows leads to more violent behavior.
4. For some people, any government action falls under the category of censorship.
5. People who are told that they cannot do something invariably want to do it.
6. Some people consider all TV programs trashy.
7. Other people say that plenty of wholesome programming is available.

D

Listen to the sentences. Underline the phrasal verbs and put a stress mark (') over the stressed word.

1. Some families are pledging to turn off their television sets for a month.
2. By not being glued to the TV set, the Smith family gains the opportunity to try out new activities.
3. The children set up a jigsaw puzzle on the kitchen table, and the whole family has been working on it each evening after dinner.
4. Mr. and Mrs. Smith started completing some projects they've been putting off for a long time.

E

Listen to each conversation. Circle the letter of the sentence below that restates the second speaker's response.

1. A: Did your children watch that violent TV program last night?
   B: No, that's impossible because we installed the V-chip.
2. A: Will I be able to install the V-chip easily?
   B: I'm quite sure you can, because if I can do it, anyone can.
3. A: What if my children try to watch forbidden programs?
   B: That would be impossible. You set the V-chip to control the programs that they watch.

4. **A:** My neighbor has a V-chip in her TV, but her children were watching a violent program last night. Do you think the V-chip stopped working?

   B: Well, I'm not sure.

5. **A:** Do you think her children figured out how to break the V-chip?

   B: Oh, no, I'm almost certain that's impossible—unless they're technical geniuses!

6. **A:** Well, those kids are pretty smart.

   B: Perhaps they are, or perhaps their mother just turned off the V-chip and wasn't supervising them very well.

Achievement Tests
Test 1 Answer Key

UNIT 1

A

[1] 1. T   2. F   3. T   4. T
[2] 1. b   2. c   3. c   4. a

B

1. b   2. e   3. d   4. a   5. c

C

1. a   3. a   5. a   7. b
2. b   4. a   6. b

D

1. hours   4. not
2. homework   5. he
3. doesn't

E

1. wasn't   4. hadn't
2. would   5. could
3. had

UNIT 2

A

[1] 1. T   2. T   3. F
[2] 1. a   2. c   3. a

B

1. a   3. a   5. b   7. a
2. b   4. a   6. a   8. b

C

1. c
2. d
3. a
4. b

D

1. c   2. b   3. a   4. c   5. d

E

1. It is preferable that a person check my Website.
2. I insist that all houses be painted white.
3. I recommend that roofs be red tile.
4. It is vital that each resident submit plans first.
5. It is essential that lawns look the same.
6. I propose that residents plant cactus.
7. I suggest (that) that person not move to my utopia.

UNIT 3

A

[1] 1. F   2. F
[2] 1. c   2. a   3. b

B

1. condescending   5. adverse
2. aloof   6. a phobia
3. an extrovert   7. merit
4. reticent   8. kindred souls

C

1. c   5. g
2. b   6. f
3. a   7. c
4. h   8. e

D

1. b   2. b   3. a

E

1. Mary, who had a problem with chronic shyness, began to attend support group meetings.
2. Mary met another woman whose interests were the same as hers.
3. Mary enjoyed attending the meetings, where she met other shy people.
4. Mary never missed her meetings, which she found very helpful.
5. Mary continued to attend the meetings and meet with her therapist, both of which helped her.
6. Mary looked forward to a time when she would feel more confident.

UNIT 4

A

1 1. T   2. F   3. F
2 1. a   2. b   3. b

B

1. b   5. e
2. a   6. d
3. g   7. f
4. c

C

1. made a splash
2. a ripple effect
3. swimming against the tide
4. triggered
5. Band-Aid solution
6. contagious idea
7. wave

D

1. transmíssion   4. theorétical
2. chaótic   5. influéntial
3. sensitívity

E

1. so afraid
2. such an important message
3. so angry
4. such careful research
5. so convinced

UNIT 5

A

1 1. T   2. F   3. T
2 1. b   2. a   3. b

B

1. b
2. a
3. c
4. f
5. e
6. d

C

1. talked . . . into   5. couldn't hurt
2. in the midst of   6. make a move
3. rise or fall   7. got into
4. scare the heck out of   8. work around

D

1. wouldn't have changed
2. should have studied
3. couldn't have made
4. must have done
5. should have done

E

1. result   4. result
2. addition   5. contrast
3. contrast

UNIT 6

A

1 1. F   2. F   3. T
2 1. c   2. a   3. a

B

1. b   2. d   3. a   4. f   5. e   6. c

C

1. foster   4. pull back
2. refrain from   5. took on
3. trace back   6. caught on

D

1. b   2. d   3. a   4. c   5. b

E

1. little   5. a few
2. few   6. a little
3. little   7. few
4. little

UNIT 7

A

1 1. T   2. F   3. T
2 1. c   2. b   3. c

B

1. b   3. c   5. a
2. f   4. e   6. d

C _____

1. fine line
2. keep tabs on
3. cheap shot
4. is all well and good
5. think twice about
6. leave . . . at the door

D _____

1. cónduct
2. suspéct
3. presént
4. objéct
5. ínsult

E _____

1. interviewing
2. to question / questioning
3. to arrive
4. performing
5. hiring
6. to videotape
7. to identify

UNIT 8

A _____

1. 1. F   2. F   3. T
2. 1. c   2. b   3. c

B _____

1. c   3. b   5. a
2. e   4. f   6. d

C _____

1. a   5. b
2. b   6. b
3. a   7. a
4. b   8. a

D _____

1. a   2. d   3. b   4. c   5. e

E _____

1. not to treat her like a child.
2. that they had just lost twenty soldiers.
3. if (whether) he (she) could send a birthday card to his (her) daughter.
4. how the Red Cross was trying to educate people.
5. that he had grown up in the anti-war culture of his generation.

UNIT 9

A _____

1. 1. F   2. T
2. 1. b   2. c   3. a

B _____

1. c   2. f   3. b   4. e   5. a   6. d

C _____

1. b   3. a   5. a   7. b
2. a   4. b   6. a   8. a

D _____

1. a   2. c   3. b   4. c

E _____

1. are convinced
2. indicates
3. are given
4. improve
5. get
6. are offered
7. include

UNIT 10

A _____

1. 1. F   2. F   2. T
2. 1. b   2. a   3. b

B _____

1. g   3. b   5. c   7. a
2. f   4. d   6. e

C _____

1. a   3. a   5. b   7. a
2. b   4. b   6. b

D _____

1. turn óff
2. try óut
3. set úp
4. putting óff

E _____

1. b   2. b   3. b   4. a   5. a   6. a

Notes

Notes

Notes

Notes

Notes

Notes

Notes

NorthStar CD Tracking Guide
Achievement Tests

TEST 1
1. Audio Program Introduction

UNIT 1
2. A. 1
3. Excerpt *(for A1 and A2)*
4. A. 2
5. B.
6. C.
7. D.
8. E.

UNIT 6
37. A. 1
38. Excerpt *(for A1 and A2)*
39. A. 2
40. B.
41. C.
42. D.
43. E.

UNIT 2
9. A. 1
10. Excerpt *(for A1 and A2)*
11. A. 2
12. B.
13. C.
14. D.
15. E.

UNIT 7
44. A. 1
45. Excerpt *(for A1 and A2)*
46. A. 2
47. B.
48. C.
49. D.
50. E.

UNIT 3
16. A. 1
17. Excerpt *(for A1 and A2)*
18. A. 2
19. B.
20. C.
21. D.
22. E.

UNIT 8
51. A. 1
52. Excerpt *(for A1 and A2)*
53. A. 2
54. B.
55. C.
56. D.
57. E.

UNIT 4
23. A. 1
24. Excerpt *(for A1 and A2)*
25. A. 2
26. B.
27. C.
28. D.
29. E.

UNIT 9
58. A. 1
59. Excerpt *(for A1 and A2)*
60. A. 2
61. B.
62. C.
63. D.
64. E.

UNIT 5
30. A. 1
31. Excerpt *(for A1 and A2)*
32. A. 2
33. B.
34. C.
35. D.
36. E.

UNIT 10
65. A. 1
66. Excerpt *(for A1 and A2)*
67. A. 2
68. B.
69. C.
70. D.
71. E.